Big Ideas from the Bible™

Old Testament Theology

Also from Mike Nappa

Bible-Smart™: Matthew

Reflections for the Grieving Soul

Welcome to BibleWorld

29 Days to Different: Love

The Promises of Jesus

Hard Way Home

VeggieTales Super Comics Volume 4

Bibleman Bible Storybook

God in Slow Motion

Instant Family Devotions

The Jesus Survey

Instant Small Group

and many more

BIG IDEAS FROM THE BIBLE™

Old Testament Theology

401 Faith-Shaping Scriptures
for Meditation, Conversation, & Transformation

Mike Nappa, Executive Editor
M.A.B.T. | M.A.E. | B.A.C.E.

WALKING CARNIVAL

Loveland, CO

BIG IDEAS FROM THE BIBLE: OLD TESTAMENT THEOLOGY
Hardcover ISBN 978-1-939953-38-4
Softcover ISBN 978-1-939953-39-1
e-Book ISBN 978-1-939953-40-7

Published by Walking Carnival
a book packaging imprint of Nappaland Communications Inc.
1437 Denver Ave. #193, Loveland, CO 80538

For a complete list of Bible translations used in this resource, and the respective permissions statements of each copyright owner, please see page 151 at the back of this book, which is an extension of this page and is dedicated to that purpose.

Executive Editor: Mike Nappa
Cover & Interior Design: WC Creative

www.WalkingCarnival.com
www.Nappaland.com

First Edition

1 2 3 4 5 6 7 • • • 2027 2026 2025 2024

"Make Readers Happy"

The Lord's word is flawless.

—Psalm 18:30 NIV

Contents

Preface: Scripture is Enough

"You have to tell them what to believe."

I had to pause for a second to make sure I'd heard correctly what my senior VP had just said. We were sitting in a publishing meeting, and I was presenting a new book I'd created. Aside from my little introduction, the entire book was a curated collection of "red-letter" quotes of Jesus making promises to his followers. Earlier, I'd privately read through the finished manuscript and found myself weeping on more than one occasion. And challenged. And grateful and hopeful and worried and all the things that go with experiencing God's Word firsthand.

My colleagues in committee were mostly supportive. I mean, how does a Christian publisher argue against printing the words of Christ? But my senior VP—let's call him William—had reservations because I'd deliberately omitted any commentary or opinion on any of the Bible passages quoted. I wanted readers to wrestle with Jesus's thoughts as a one-on-one experience, to let the Holy Spirit work without any interference from me.

That didn't sit well with William.

"You have to tell them what to believe," he objected. "Otherwise readers won't believe the right thing."

Now, don't get me wrong. I'm all for teaching the Bible, and preaching and commentaries, and Bible background, and theological accuracy, and being a person "who correctly handles the word of truth" (2 Timothy 2:15 NIV). In fact, I have a seminary degree myself, and can never seem to resist adding a new Scripture reference book to the hundreds already littering my shelves.

BUT ...

Telling readers what to believe wasn't the point of that particular book. The idea was to give people the words of Jesus—and then (with the Holy Spirit's influence) let them decide what they were going to do with them. I looked at my friend and VP across the table, and all I could think to say was,

"I believe Scripture is enough."

To William's credit, he allowed the book to be published even though he disagreed with me. But I've thought about that moment a lot in the time that's passed since then. It frequently made me wonder:

Why are we so often afraid to let Scripture speak for itself?

Some Time Later ...

I went back to my home office thinking about a book in my writing files on "big ideas" in the Bible. What would happen, I wondered, if I just eliminated my denominational preferences and theological opinions and mistaken assumptions, and only quoted relevant Scriptures instead? If I made a table of contents highlighting major theological themes of Scripture—and then let the Bible do the talking in each chapter instead of me?

Finally, I took a deep breath, opened up my Old Testament, and decided to find out. The result is this book that you now hold in your hands.

What's Inside This Book

There are a few things I should tell you about what follows in here.

First, the Old Testament Scriptures quoted are not theologically exhaustive, but representative instead. That means for each "big idea" section in this book, I've selected between 18 to 30 Bible passages that are meaningful to that topic (and to me)—but not every Old Testament verse on the subject. Constraints in space and time and biblical literary styles prevented that, and besides, there are plenty of concordances and online search engines already available to you if you're looking for a comprehensive list like that.

Second, I've provided reference notations for each Scripture verse included in here so that you can easily find them in your own Bible—but I've typically only quoted the relevant sections from each reference. So, for instance, one quote may include an entire Bible verse, while others may highlight only the first half of a verse, or the last portion, or the middle. That way you can concentrate on the sections of Scripture that are most applicable to the "big idea" being discussed—but still see where to find it in its original context within your own copy of the Bible. If you find something particularly interesting, I'd encourage you to look up that verse in full in your Bible.

Third, feel free to approach this collection in whatever way is most meaningful for you.

- Some will want to start at the beginning and read through to the end.
- Others will prefer to skip around from chapter to chapter, drinking in Scripture topically as it relates to current theological interest.
- Many will want to join with others to talk through these Bible verses—in coffee clubs or small group studies or couples' devotions or family dinners.
- You may even want to pray each verse privately, journaling it to fit your life and spiritual desires.

All of these approaches are OK—even encouraged. After all, when your heart is set on God's Word and the Holy Spirit gets involved, anything can happen!

All right. You're ready.

So this is now my prayer for you:

May Scripture be enough for God's Spirit to meet you firsthand today, as you dig deeply, and frequently, into His Word collected in the pages of *Big Ideas from the Bible: Old Testament Theology*. Amen!

Mike Nappa, Executive Editor
M.A.B.T. | M.A.E. | B.A.C.E.

Big Idea #1

Who Is God?

She gave this name to the Lord who spoke to her: "You are the God who sees me," for she said, "I have now seen the One who sees me."

—Genesis 16:13 NIV

\\\

God replied to Moses, "I AM WHO I AM. Say this to the people of Israel: I AM has sent me to you."

God also said to Moses, "Say this to the people of Israel: Yahweh, the God of your ancestors—the God of Abraham, the God of Isaac, and the God of Jacob—has sent me to you.

This is my eternal name, my name to remember for all generations.

—Exodus 3:14-15 NLT

///

The Lord is my strength and song,
And He has become my salvation;
He is my God, and I will praise Him;
My father's God, and I will exalt Him.

—Exodus 15:2 NKJV

\\\

Who is like you, O Lord, among the gods? Who is like you?—majestic in holiness, fearful in praises, working wonders?

—Exodus 15:11 NET

///

The Lord passed in front of Moses, calling out, "Yahweh! The Lord! The God of compassion and mercy! I am slow to anger and filled with unfailing love and faithfulness.

—Exodus 34:6 NLT

\\\

God is not man, that he should lie, or a son of man, that he should change his mind. Has he said, and will he not do it? Or has he spoken, and will he not fulfill it?

—Numbers 23:19 ESV

///

For the Lord your God is a consuming fire, a jealous God.

—Deuteronomy 4:24 NASB

\\\

For the Lord your God is God of gods and Lord of lords, the great God, mighty and awesome, who shows no partiality nor takes a bribe.

—Deuteronomy 10:17 NKJV

///

Lord, the God of the heavens, the great and awe-inspiring God who keeps his gracious covenant with those who love him and keep his commands.

—Nehemiah 1:5 CSB

///

As for God, his way is perfect:
The Lord's word is flawless; he shields all who take refuge in him.

—Psalm 18:30 NIV

\\\

The Lord is my shepherd; I shall not want.
He maketh me to lie down in green pastures: he leadeth me beside the still waters. He restoreth my soul: he leadeth me in the paths of righteousness for his name's sake.

—Psalm 23:1-3 KJV

///

Sing a song of wisdom, for God is King of the whole earth.

—Psalm 47:7 CSB

\\\

God is my helper; the Lord is the sustainer of my life.

—Psalm 54:4 CSB

\\\

A father to the fatherless, a defender of widows, is God in his holy dwelling.

—Psalm 68:5 NIV

///

God, your way is holy. What god is great like God? You are the God who works wonders; you revealed your strength among the peoples.

—Psalm 77:13-14 CSB

\\\

Let them know that you, whose name is the Lord—that you alone are the Most High over all the earth.

—Psalm 83:18 NIV

///

For you, O Lord, are good and forgiving, abounding in steadfast love to all who call on you ... You, O Lord, are a God merciful and gracious, slow to anger and abounding in steadfast love and faithfulness.

—Psalm 86:5, 15 NRSV

\\\

How kind the Lord is! How good he is! So merciful, this God of ours!

—Psalm 116:5 NLT

///

Our help is in the name of the Lord, who made heaven and earth.

—Psalm 124:8 KJV

\\\

Lord, you have searched me and known me. You know when I sit down and when I stand up; you understand my thoughts from far away. You observe my travels and my rest; you are aware of all my ways. Before a word is on my tongue, you know all about it, Lord. You have encircled me; you have placed your hand on me. This wondrous knowledge is beyond me. It is lofty; I am unable to reach it.

—Psalm 139:1-6 CSB

///

The name of the Lord is a strong tower; The righteous run to it and are safe.

—Proverbs 18:10 NKJV

\\\

For the Lord is our judge, the Lord is our lawgiver, the Lord is our king; he will save us.

—Isaiah 33:22 KJV

///

With whom will you compare God?
What likeness will you set up for comparison with him? …

Do you not know? Have you not heard? Has it not been declared to you from the beginning? Have you not considered the foundations of the earth? God is enthroned above the circle of the earth; its inhabitants are like grasshoppers. He stretches out the heavens like thin cloth and spreads them out like a tent to live in. He reduces princes to nothing and makes judges of the earth like a wasteland. They are barely planted, barely sown, their stem hardly takes root in the ground when he blows on them and they wither, and a whirlwind carries them away like stubble.

"To whom will you compare me, or who is my equal?" asks the Holy One. Look up and see! Who created these? He brings out the stars by number; he calls all of them by name. Because of his great power and strength, not one of them is missing …

Do you not know? Have you not heard? The Lord is the everlasting God, the Creator of the whole earth. He never becomes faint or weary; there is no limit to his understanding.

—Isaiah 40:18, 21-26, 28 CSB

\\\

For I, the Lord your God, hold your right hand; it is I who say to you, "Fear not, I am the one who helps you."

—Isaiah 41:13 ESV

///

This is what the Lord, the King of Israel and its Redeemer, the Lord of Armies, says: I am the first and I am the last. There is no God but me.

—Isaiah 44:6 CSB

\\\

But now, O Lord, You are our Father, We are the clay, and You our potter; And all of us are the work of Your hand.

—Isaiah 64:8 NASB

///

But the Lord is the true God, he is the living God, and an everlasting king: at his wrath the earth shall tremble, and the nations shall not be able to abide his indignation.

—Jeremiah 10:10 KJV

\\\

Behold, I am the Lord, the God of all flesh:
is there any thing too hard for me?

—Jeremiah 32:27 KJV

///

I make a decree, that in all my royal dominion people should tremble and fear before the God of Daniel: For he is the living God, enduring forever. His kingdom shall never be destroyed, and his dominion has no end.

—Daniel 6:26 NRSV

\\\

There is no other God like you! You forgive sin and pardon the rebellion of those who remain among your people. You do not remain angry forever, but delight in showing loyal love.

—Micah 7:18 NET

Big Idea #2

Jesus, The Messiah

I will put hostility between you and the woman, and between your offspring and her offspring. He will strike your head, and you will strike his heel.

—Genesis 3:15 CSB
(xref: Hebrews 2:14; 1 John 3:8)

\\\

Abraham is to become a great and powerful nation, and all the nations of the earth will be blessed through him.

—Genesis 18:18 CSB
(xref: Galatians 3:8-9)

///

The scepter will not depart from Judah, nor the ruler's staff from between his feet, until he to whom it belongs shall come and the obedience of the nations shall be his.

—Genesis 49:10 NIV
(xref: John 18:33-37; Hebrews 1:2-4; Revelation 17:14)

\\\

Moses continued, "The Lord your God will raise up for you a prophet like me from among your fellow Israelites. You must listen to him."

—Deuteronomy 18:15 NLT
(xref: Luke 7:16-17, 24:19)

///

The kings of the earth take their stand, and the rulers conspire together against the Lord and his Anointed One.

—Psalm 2:2 CSB
(xref: Luke 23:1-12, 24:20, 25-27)

\\\

I will proclaim the Lord's decree: He said to me, "You are my son; today I have become your father.

—Psalm 2:7 NIV
(xref: Luke 1:31-32; John 3:16)

///

No wonder my heart is glad, and I rejoice. My body rests in safety. For you will not leave my soul among the dead or allow your holy one to rot in the grave.

—Psalm 16:9-10 NASB
(xref: Luke 24:1-6; Acts 13:29-30)

\\\

All who see me mock me; they hurl insults, shaking their heads.

—Psalm 22:7 NIV
(xref: Matthew 27:39-42)

///

My enemies surround me like a pack of dogs; an evil gang closes in on me. They have pierced my hands and feet.

—Psalm 22:16 NLT
(xref: Luke 23:35; John 19:17-18)

\\\

Even my friend in whom I trusted, one who ate my bread, has raised his heel against me.

—Psalm 41:9 CSB
(xref: Luke 22:3-4, 47-48)

///

For zeal for your house has consumed me, and the reproaches of those who reproach you have fallen on me.

—Psalm 69:9 ESV
(xref: John 2:13-17)

\\\

The Lord said, "I have made a covenant with my chosen one; I have made a promise on oath to David, my servant: 'I will give you an eternal dynasty and establish your throne throughout future generations.'"

—Psalm 89:3-4 NET
(xref: Luke 1:30-33; Acts 7:55)

///

Therefore the Lord himself shall give you a sign; Behold, a virgin shall conceive, and bear a son, and shall call his name Immanuel.

—Isaiah 7:14 KJV
(xref: Matthew 1:20-23)

\\\

Nevertheless, that time of darkness and despair will not go on forever. The land of Zebulun and Naphtali will be humbled, but there will be a time in the future when Galilee of the Gentiles, which lies along the road that runs between the Jordan and the sea, will be filled with glory.

The people who walk in darkness will see a great light. For those who live in a land of deep darkness, a light will shine.

—Isaiah 9:1-2 NLT
(xref: Luke 2:25-33; John 1:4-5)

///

For unto us a child is born, unto us a son is given: and the government shall be upon his shoulder: and his name shall be called Wonderful, Counsellor, The mighty God, The everlasting Father, The Prince of Peace.

—Isaiah 9:6 KJV
(xref: Matthew 28:18; Hebrews 1:3)

\\\

And the spirit of the Lord shall rest upon him, the spirit of wisdom and understanding, the spirit of counsel and might, the spirit of knowledge and of the fear of the Lord.

—Isaiah 11:2 KJV
(xref: Mark 1:9-11)

///

Then the eyes of the blind shall be opened,
and the ears of the deaf shall be unstopped.

—Isaiah 35:5 KJV
(xref: Mark 7:31-37, 10:46-52)

\\\

Many people were shocked when they saw him. His appearance was so damaged he did not look like a man; his form was so changed they could barely tell he was human.

—Isaiah 52:14 NCV
(xref: John 19:1-3)

///

He is despised and rejected of men; a man of sorrows, and acquainted with grief: and we hid as it were our faces from him; he was despised, and we esteemed him not.

—Isaiah 53:3 KJV
(xref: Mark 14:32-42, 15:16-20)

\\\

Surely he hath borne our griefs, and carried our sorrows: yet we did esteem him stricken, smitten of God, and afflicted.

—Isaiah 53:4 KJV
(xref: Mark 15:27-32)

///

But he was wounded for our transgressions, he was bruised for our iniquities: the chastisement of our peace was upon him; and with his stripes we are healed.

—Isaiah 53:5 KJV
(xref: 1 Corinthians 15:3; 1 Peter 2:24)

\\\

He was oppressed, and he was afflicted, yet he opened not his mouth: he is brought as a lamb to the slaughter, and as a sheep before her shearers is dumb, so he openeth not his mouth.

—Isaiah 53:7 KJV
(xref: Matthew 27:12-14; Acts 8:32-35)

///

Therefore I will give him a portion among the great, and he will divide the spoils with the strong, because he poured out his life unto death, and was numbered with the transgressors. For he bore the sin of many, and made intercession for the transgressors.

—Isaiah 53:12 NIV
(xref: Romans 5:6-10; 2 Corinthians 5:21)

\\\

The Spirit of the Lord God is upon me, because the Lord has anointed me to bring good news to the poor; he has sent me to bind up the brokenhearted, to proclaim liberty to the captives, and the opening of the prison to those who are bound.

—Isaiah 61:1 ESV
(xref: Matthew 11:2-5; Luke 4:16-21)

///

When Israel was a child, then I loved him, and called my son out of Egypt.

—Hosea 11:1 KJV
(xref: Matthew 2:13-15)

\\\

But you, O Bethlehem Ephrathah, who are too little to be among the clans of Judah, from you shall come forth for me one who is to be ruler in Israel, whose coming forth is from of old, from ancient days.

—Micah 5:2 ESV
(xref: Matthew 2:1-6; Luke 2:4-7)

///

Rejoice greatly, O daughter of Zion! Shout in triumph, O daughter of Jerusalem! Behold, your king is coming to you; He is just and endowed with salvation, Humble, and mounted on a donkey, Even on a colt, the foal of a donkey.

—Zechariah 9:9 NASB
(xref: John 12:12-16)

Big Idea #3

Holy Spirit

In the beginning God created the heaven and the earth. And the earth was without form, and void; and darkness was upon the face of the deep. And the Spirit of God moved upon the face of the waters…

—Genesis 1:1-2 KJV

\\\

And Pharaoh said unto his servants, Can we find such a one as this is, a man in whom the Spirit of God is?

—Genesis 41:38 KJV

///

Look, I have appointed by name Bezalel son of Uri, son of Hur, of the tribe of Judah. I have filled him with God's Spirit, with wisdom, understanding, and ability in every craft.

—Exodus 31:2-3 CSB

\\\

The Spirit of the Lord entered Samson with great power, and he tore the lion apart with his bare hands. For him it was as easy as tearing apart a young goat. But Samson did not tell his father or mother what he had done…

Then the Spirit of the Lord entered Samson and gave him great power. Samson went down to the city of Ashkelon and killed thirty of its men and took all that they had and gave the clothes to the men who had answered his riddle. Then he went to his father's house very angry.

—Judges 14:6, 19 NCV

///

When Samson came to the place named Lehi, the Philistines came to meet him, shouting for joy. Then the Spirit of the Lord entered Samson and gave him great power. The ropes on him weakened like burned strings and fell off his hands!

—Judges 15:14 NCV

\\\

When Saul and his servant arrived at Gibeah, a group of prophets met him. Then the Spirit of God came powerfully on him, and he prophesied along with them.

—1 Samuel 10:10 CSB

///

So Samuel took the horn full of olive oil and anointed him in the presence of his brothers. The Spirit of the Lord rushed upon David from that day onward. Then Samuel got up and went to Ramah.

—1 Samuel 16:13 NET

\\\

You sent your good Spirit to instruct them. You did not withhold your manna from their mouths, and you gave them water for their thirst…

You were patient with them for many years, and your Spirit warned them through your prophets, but they would not listen. Therefore, you handed them over to the surrounding peoples.

—Nehemiah 9:20, 30 CSB

///

The Spirit of God has made me, and the breath of the Almighty gives me life.

—Job 33:4 CSB

\\\

If God were to take back his spirit and withdraw his breath, all life would cease, and humanity would turn again to dust.

—Job 34:14-15 NLT

///

Do not cast me away from your presence, and do not take your holy spirit from me.

—Psalm 51:11 NRSV

\\\

When you send your Spirit, they are created, and you renew the face of the ground.

—Psalm 104:30 NIV

///

Where can I go to escape your Spirit? Where can I flee from your presence? If I go up to heaven, you are there; if I make my bed in Sheol, you are there. If I live at the eastern horizon or settle at the western limits, even there your hand will lead me; your right hand will hold on to me.

—Psalm 139:7-10 CSB

\\\

Teach me to do Your will, For You are my God; Let Your good Spirit lead me on level ground.

—Psalm 143:10 NASB

///

And the spirit of the Lord shall rest upon him, the spirit of wisdom and understanding, the spirit of counsel and might, the spirit of knowledge and of the fear of the Lord.

—Isaiah 11:2 KJV

\\\

This will continue until God pours his Spirit from above upon us. Then the desert will be like a fertile field and the fertile field like a forest. Justice will be found even in the desert, and fairness will be found in the fertile fields.

—Isaiah 32:15-16 NCV

///

For I will pour water on the thirsty land, and streams on the dry ground; I will pour out my Spirit on your offspring, and my blessing on your descendants. They will spring up like grass in a meadow, like poplar trees by flowing streams.

—Isaiah 44:3-4 NIV

\\\

"As for Me," says the Lord, "this is My covenant with them: My Spirit who is upon you, and My words which I have put in your mouth, shall not depart from your mouth, nor from the mouth of your descendants, nor from the mouth of your descendants' descendants," says the Lord, "from this time and forevermore."

—Isaiah 59:21 NKJV

///

The Spirit of the Lord God is upon me, because the Lord has anointed me to bring good news to the poor; he has sent me to bind up the brokenhearted, to proclaim liberty to the captives, and the opening of the prison to those who are bound.

—Isaiah 61:1 ESV

\\\

Like cattle that go down into the valley, the Spirit of the Lord gave them rest. You led your people this way to make a glorious name for yourself.

—Isaiah 63:14 CSB

///

I will give you a new heart and put a new spirit within you; I will take the heart of stone out of your flesh and give you a heart of flesh. I will put My Spirit within you and cause you to walk in My statutes, and you will keep My judgments and do them.

—Ezekiel 36:26-27 NKJV

\\\

"I will put My Spirit within you and you will come to life, and I will place you on your own land. Then you will know that I, the Lord, have spoken and done it," declares the Lord.

—Ezekiel 37:14 NASB

///

"They will know that I am the Lord their God when I regather them to their own land after having exiled them among the nations. I will leave none of them behind. I will no longer hide my face from them, for I will pour out my Spirit on the house of Israel." This is the declaration of the Lord God.

—Ezekiel 39:28-29 CSB

\\\

And afterward, I will pour out my Spirit on all people. Your sons and daughters will prophesy, your old men will dream dreams, your young men will see visions. Even on my servants, both men and women, I will pour out my Spirit in those days.

—Joel 2:28-29 NIV

///

But as for me, I am filled with power, with the Spirit of the Lord, and with justice and might, to declare to Jacob his transgression and to Israel his sin.

—Micah 3:8 ESV

\\\

This is the promise I made to you when you came out of Egypt, and my Spirit is present among you; don't be afraid.

—Haggai 2:5 CSB

///

Then he said to me, "This is the word of the Lord to Zerubbabel: Not by might, nor by power, but by my Spirit, says the Lord of hosts.

—Zechariah 4:6 ESV

Big Idea #4

The Love of God

In Your lovingkindness You have led the people whom You have redeemed; In Your strength You have guided them to Your holy habitation.

—Exodus 15:13 NASB

\\\

The Lord passed in front of Moses, calling out, "Yahweh! The Lord! The God of compassion and mercy! I am slow to anger and filled with unfailing love and faithfulness.

—Exodus 34:6 NLT

///

It is not because you were more numerous than all the other peoples that the Lord favored and chose you—for in fact you were the least numerous of all peoples. Rather it is because of his love for you and his faithfulness to the promise he solemnly vowed to your ancestors that the Lord brought you out with great power, redeeming you from the place of slavery, from the power of Pharaoh king of Egypt …

He will love and bless you, and make you numerous. He will bless you with many children, with the produce of your soil, your grain, your new wine, your oil, the offspring of your oxen, and the young of your flocks in the land which he promised your ancestors to give you.

—Deuteronomy 7:7-8, 13 NET

\\\

He administers justice for the fatherless and the widow, and loves the stranger, giving him food and clothing.

—Deuteronomy 10:18 NKJV

///

The Lord your God turned the curse into a blessing for you, because the Lord your God loved you.

—Deuteronomy 23:5 ESV

\\\

Oh give thanks to the Lord, for he is good; for his steadfast love endures forever!

—1 Chronicles 16:34 ESV

///

They refused to listen, And did not remember Your wondrous deeds which You had performed among them; So they became stubborn and appointed a leader to return to their slavery in Egypt. But You are a God of forgiveness, Gracious and compassionate, Slow to anger and abounding in lovingkindness; And You did not forsake them.

—Nehemiah 9:17 NASB

\\\

Wicked people have many troubles, but the Lord's love surrounds those who trust him.

—Psalm 32:10 NCV

///

Your love, Lord, reaches to the heavens, your faithfulness to the skies.

Your righteousness is like the highest mountains, your justice like the great deep.

You, Lord, preserve both people and animals. How priceless is your unfailing love, O God! People take refuge in the shadow of your wings.

—Psalm 36:5-7 NIV

\\\

Yet the Lord will command his lovingkindness in the day time, and in the night his song shall be with me, and my prayer unto the God of my life.

—Psalm 42:8 KJV

///

Because Your lovingkindness is better than life,
My lips shall praise You.

—Psalm 63:3 NKJV

\\\

The Lord is merciful and gracious, slow to anger and abounding in steadfast love. He will not always chide, nor will he keep his anger forever. He does not deal with us according to our sins, nor repay us according to our iniquities.

—Psalm 103:8-10 ESV

///

As a father has compassion on his children, so the Lord has compassion on those who fear him.

—Psalm 103:13 CSB

\\\

But the steadfast love of the Lord is from everlasting to everlasting on those who fear him, and his righteousness to children's children.

—Psalm 103:17 ESV

///

Hallelujah! Give thanks to the Lord, for he is good; his faithful love endures forever.

—Psalm 106:1 CSB

\\\

Who is wise? Let him give heed to these things, And consider the lovingkindnesses of the Lord.

—Psalm 107:43 NASB

///

He has caused his wondrous works to be remembered. The Lord is gracious and compassionate.

—Psalm 111:4 CSB

\\\

Give thanks to the Lord, for he is good.
His faithful love endures forever.
Give thanks to the God of gods.
His faithful love endures forever.
Give thanks to the Lord of lords.
His faithful love endures forever.
He alone does great wonders.
His faithful love endures forever.
He made the heavens skillfully.
His faithful love endures forever.
He spread the land on the waters.
His faithful love endures forever.
He made the great lights:
His faithful love endures forever.
the sun to rule by day,
His faithful love endures forever.
the moon and stars to rule by night.
His faithful love endures forever.
He struck the firstborn of the Egyptians
His faithful love endures forever.
and brought Israel out from among them
His faithful love endures forever.
with a strong hand and outstretched arm.
His faithful love endures forever.
He divided the Red Sea
His faithful love endures forever.
and led Israel through,
His faithful love endures forever.
but hurled Pharaoh and his army into the Red Sea.
His faithful love endures forever.
He led his people in the wilderness.
His faithful love endures forever.
He struck down great kings
His faithful love endures forever.
and slaughtered famous kings—
His faithful love endures forever.
Sihon king of the Amorites
His faithful love endures forever.

and Og king of Bashan—
His faithful love endures forever.
and gave their land as an inheritance,
His faithful love endures forever.
an inheritance to Israel his servant.
His faithful love endures forever.
He remembered us in our humiliation
His faithful love endures forever.
and rescued us from our foes.
His faithful love endures forever.
He gives food to every creature.
His faithful love endures forever.
Give thanks to the God of heaven!
His faithful love endures forever.

—Psalm 136 CSB

///

I will bow down toward your holy temple and give thanks to your name for your constant love and truth. You have exalted your name and your promise above everything else.

—Psalm 138:2 CSB

\\\

Let me hear of your unfailing love each morning, for I am trusting you. Show me where to walk, for I give myself to you.

—Psalm 143:8 NLT

///

The Lord is gracious, and full of compassion; slow to anger, and of great mercy. The Lord is good to all: and his tender mercies are over all his works.

—Psalm 145:8-9 KJV

\\\

In love you have delivered my life from the pit of destruction, for you have cast all my sins behind your back.

—Isaiah 38:17 ESV

\\\

I will tell of the Lord's unfailing love. I will praise the Lord for all he has done. I will rejoice in his great goodness to Israel, which he has granted according to his mercy and love.

—Isaiah 63:7 NLT

///

I have loved you with an everlasting love; therefore, I have continued to extend faithful love to you.

—Jeremiah 31:3 CSB

\\\

It is of the Lord's mercies that we are not consumed, because his compassions fail not. They are new every morning: great is thy faithfulness.

—Lamentations 3:22-23 KJV

///

Return to the Lord, your God, for he is gracious and merciful, slow to anger, and abounding in steadfast love, and relents from punishing.

—Joel 2:13 NRSV

\\\

You are a gracious and compassionate God, slow to anger, abounding in faithful love, and one who relents from sending disaster.

—Jonah 4:2 CSB

Big Idea #5

Creation

In the beginning God created the heaven and the earth.

—Genesis 1:1 KJV

\\\

Then God said, "Let the earth produce vegetation: seed-bearing plants and fruit trees on the earth bearing fruit with seed in it according to their kinds." And it was so …
Then God said, "Let there be lights in the expanse of the sky to separate the day from the night. They will serve as signs for seasons and for days and years. They will be lights in the expanse of the sky to provide light on the earth." And it was so …
Then God said, "Let the water swarm with living creatures, and let birds fly above the earth across the expanse of the sky." So God created the large sea-creatures and every living creature that moves and swarms in the water, according to their kinds. He also created every winged creature according to its kind. And God saw that it was good …
Then God said, "Let the earth produce living creatures according to their kinds: livestock, creatures that crawl, and the wildlife of the earth according to their kinds." And it was so.

—Genesis 1:11, 14-15, 20-21, 24 CSB

///

Then God said, "Let us make humankind in our image, according to our likeness; and let them have dominion over the fish of the sea, and over the birds of the air, and over the cattle, and over all the wild animals of the earth, and over every creeping thing that creeps upon the earth." So God created humankind in his image, in the image of God he created them; male and female he created them.

—Genesis 1:26-27 NRSV

\\\

Then the Lord asked Moses, "Who makes a person's mouth? Who decides whether people speak or do not speak, hear or do not hear, see or do not see? Is it not I, the Lord?

—Exodus 4:11 NLT

///

For in six days the Lord made the heavens, the earth, the sea, and everything in them; but on the seventh day he rested.

—Exodus 20:11 NLT

\\\

The Lord brings death and makes alive; he brings down to the grave and raises up. The Lord sends poverty and wealth; he humbles and he exalts. He raises the poor from the dust and lifts the needy from the ash heap; he seats them with princes and has them inherit a throne of honor.

For the foundations of the earth are the Lord's; on them he has set the world.

—1 Samuel 2:6-8 NIV

///

You are the Lord, you alone. You have made heaven, the heaven of heavens, with all their host, the earth and all that is on it, the seas and all that is in them; and you preserve all of them; and the host of heaven worships you.

—Nehemiah 9:6 ESV

\\\

But ask the animals, and they will teach you; the birds of the air, and they will tell you; ask the plants of the earth, and they will teach you; and the fish of the sea will declare to you.

Who among all these does not know that the hand of the Lord has done this? In his hand is the life of every living thing and the breath of every human being.

—Job 12:7-10 NRSV

///

Get ready to answer me like a man; when I question you, you will inform me.

Where were you when I established the earth? Tell me, if you have understanding. Who fixed its dimensions? Certainly you know! Who stretched a measuring line across it? What supports its foundations? Or who laid its cornerstone while the morning stars sang together and all the sons of God shouted for joy?

Who enclosed the sea behind doors when it burst from the womb, when I made the clouds its garment and total darkness its blanket, when I determined its boundaries and put its bars and doors in place, when I declared: "You may come this far, but no farther; your proud waves stop here"?

Have you ever in your life commanded the morning or assigned the dawn its place, so it may seize the edges of the earth and shake the wicked out of it? …

Have you traveled to the sources of the sea or walked in the depths of the oceans? Have the gates of death been revealed to you? Have you seen the gates of deep darkness? Have you comprehended the extent of the earth? Tell me, if you know all this. …

Can you fasten the chains of the Pleiades or loosen the belt of Orion?

Can you bring out the constellations in their season and lead the Bear and her cubs? Do you know the laws of heaven?

Can you impose its authority on earth? Can you command the clouds so that a flood of water covers you? Can you send out lightning bolts, and they go? Do they report to you: "Here we are"?

Who put wisdom in the heart or gave the mind understanding?

. . .

Will the one who contends with the Almighty correct him? Let him who argues with God give an answer.

—Job 38:3-13, 16-18, 31-36, 40:2 CSB

\\\

Then Job replied to the Lord:

I know that you can do anything and no plan of yours can be thwarted. You asked, "Who is this who conceals my counsel with ignorance?" Surely I spoke about things I did not understand, things too wondrous for me to know.

—Job 42:1-3 CSB

///

The heavens declare the glory of God; the sky displays his handiwork.

—Psalm 19:1 NET

\\\

The earth and everything in it, the world and its inhabitants, belong to the Lord; for he laid its foundation on the seas and established it.

—Psalm 24:1-2 CSB

///

For with you is the fountain of life; in your light we see light.

—Psalm 36:9 NRSV

\\\

Know that the Lord, He is God; It is He who has made us, and not we ourselves; We are His people and the sheep of His pasture.

—Psalm 100:3 NKJV

///

You set the earth on its foundations, so that it shall never be shaken. You cover it with the deep as with a garment; the waters stood above the mountains. At your rebuke they flee; at the sound of your thunder they take to flight. They rose up to the mountains, ran down to the valleys to the place that you appointed for them. You set a boundary that they may not pass, so that they might not again cover the earth. You make springs gush forth in the valleys; they flow between the hills.

—Psalm 104:5-10 NRSV

\\\

For it was you who created my inward parts; you knit me together in my mother's womb. I will praise you because I have been remarkably and wondrously made. Your works are wondrous, and I know this very well. My bones were not hidden from you when I was made in secret, when I was formed in the depths of the earth. Your eyes saw me when I was formless; all my days were written in your book and planned before a single one of them began.

—Psalm 139:13-16 CSB

///

Just as you don't know the path of the wind, or how bones develop in the womb of a pregnant woman, so also you don't know the work of God who makes everything.

—Ecclesiastes 11:5 CSB

\\\

Look up and see! Who created these? He brings out the stars by number; he calls all of them by name. Because of his great power and strength, not one of them is missing …

Do you not know? Have you not heard? The Lord is the everlasting God, the Creator of the whole earth. He never becomes faint or weary; there is no limit to his understanding.

—Isaiah 40:26, 28 CSB

///

This is what the Lord, your Redeemer who formed you from the womb, says: I am the Lord, who made everything; who stretched out the heavens by myself; who alone spread out the earth

—Isaiah 44:24 CSB

\\\

I form the light, and create darkness: I make peace, and create evil: I the Lord do all these things.

—Isaiah 45:7 KJV

///

But now, O Lord, You are our Father, We are the clay, and You our potter; And all of us are the work of Your hand.

—Isaiah 64:8 NASB

\\\

It is I who by my great power and my outstretched arm have made the earth, with the people and animals that are on the earth, and I give it to whomever I please.

—Jeremiah 27:5 NRSV

///

For behold, He who forms mountains and creates the wind And declares to man what are His thoughts, He who makes dawn into darkness And treads on the high places of the earth, The Lord God of hosts is His name.

—Amos 4:13 NASB

\\\

It is the Lord who created the stars, the Pleiades and Orion. He turns darkness into morning and day into night. He draws up water from the oceans and pours it down as rain on the land. The Lord is his name!

—Amos 5:8 NLT

Big Idea #6

The Spiritual Realm

After God forced humans out of the garden, he placed angels and a sword of fire that flashed around in every direction on its eastern border. This kept people from getting to the tree of life.

—Genesis 3:24 NCV

\\\

Then he dreamed, and behold, a ladder was set up on the earth, and its top reached to heaven; and there the angels of God were ascending and descending on it.

—Genesis 28:12 NKJV

///

I am sending an angel ahead of you, who will protect you as you travel. He will lead you to the place I have prepared. Pay attention to the angel and obey him. Do not turn against him; he will not forgive such turning against him because my power is in him. If you listen carefully to all he says and do everything that I tell you, I will be an enemy to your enemies. I will fight all who fight against you. My angel will go ahead of you and take you into the land of the Amorites, Hittites, Perizzites, Canaanites, Hivites, and Jebusites, and I will destroy them.

—Exodus 23:20-23 NCV

\\\

They sacrificed to demons, not God, to deities they had never known, to new ones recently arrived, whom your ancestors had not feared.

—Deuteronomy 32:17 NRSV

///

Micaiah said, "Therefore, hear the word of the Lord. I saw the Lord sitting on His throne, and all the host of heaven standing by Him on His right and on His left. The Lord said, 'Who will entice Ahab to go up and fall at Ramoth-gilead?' And one said this while another said that. Then a spirit came forward and stood before the Lord and said, 'I will entice him.' The Lord said to him, 'How?' And he said, 'I will go out and be a deceiving spirit in the mouth of all his prophets.' Then He said, 'You are to entice him and also prevail. Go and do so.' Now therefore, behold, the Lord has put a deceiving spirit in the mouth of all these your prophets; and the Lord has proclaimed disaster against you."

—1 Kings 22:19-23 NASB

\\\

That night the angel of the Lord went out to the Assyrian camp and killed 185,000 Assyrian soldiers. When the surviving Assyrians woke up the next morning, they found corpses everywhere.

—2 Kings 19:35 NLT

///

When David looked up and saw the angel of the Lord standing between earth and heaven, with his drawn sword in his hand stretched out over Jerusalem, David and the elders, clothed in sackcloth, fell facedown.

—1 Chronicles 21:16 CSB

\\\

One day the heavenly beings came to present themselves before the Lord, and Satan also came among them. The Lord said to Satan, "Where have you come from?" Satan answered the Lord, "From going to and fro on the earth, and from walking up and down on it."

—Job 1:6-7 NRSV

///

But why are people even important to you? Why do you take care of human beings? You made them a little lower than the angels and crowned them with glory and honor.

—Psalm 8:4-5 NCV

\\\

O Lord, the heavens praise your amazing deeds, as well as your faithfulness in the angelic assembly. For who in the skies can compare to the Lord? Who is like the Lord among the heavenly beings, a God who is honored in the great angelic assembly, and more awesome than all who surround him?

—Psalm 89:5-7 NET

///

He has put his angels in charge of you to watch over you wherever you go. They will catch you in their hands so that you will not hit your foot on a rock.

—Psalm 91:11-12 NCV

\\\

Bless the Lord, all his angels of great strength, who do his word, obedient to his command.

—Psalm 103:20 CSB

///

They served their idols, which became a snare to them. They sacrificed their sons and daughters to demons. They shed innocent blood—the blood of their sons and daughters whom they sacrificed to the idols of Canaan; so the land became polluted with blood.

—Psalm 106:36-38 CSB

\\\

In the year that King Uzziah died, I saw the Lord sitting on a throne, high and lifted up, and the train of His robe filled the temple. Above it stood seraphim; each one had six wings: with two he covered his face, with two he covered his feet, and with two he flew. And one cried to another and said:

"Holy, holy, holy is the Lord of hosts; The whole earth is full of His glory!"

And the posts of the door were shaken by the voice of him who cried out, and the house was filled with smoke.

—Isaiah 6:1-4 NKJV

///

How you are fallen from heaven, O Lucifer, son of the morning! How you are cut down to the ground, You who weakened the nations! For you have said in your heart: 'I will ascend into heaven, I will exalt my throne above the stars of God; I will also sit on the mount of the congregation On the farthest sides of the north; I will ascend above the heights of the clouds, I will be like the Most High.' Yet you shall be brought down to Sheol, To the lowest depths of the Pit.

—Isaiah 14:12-15 NKJV

\\\

I ordained and anointed you as the mighty angelic guardian. You had access to the holy mountain of God and walked among the stones of fire.

You were blameless in all you did from the day you were created until the day evil was found in you. Your rich commerce led you to violence, and you sinned. So I banished you in disgrace from the mountain of God. I expelled you, O mighty guardian, from your place among the stones of fire. Your heart was filled with pride because of all your beauty. Your wisdom was corrupted by your love of splendor. So I threw you to the ground and exposed you to the curious gaze of kings.

—Ezekiel 28:14-17 NLT

///

My God sent his angel and closed the lions' mouths so that they have not harmed me, because I was found to be innocent before him. Nor have I done any harm to you, O king.

—Daniel 6:22 NET

\\\

On the twenty-fourth day of the first month, as I was standing on the bank of the great river, the Tigris, I looked up, and there was a man dressed in linen, with a belt of gold from Uphaz around his waist. His body was like beryl, his face like the brilliance of lightning, his eyes like flaming torches, his arms and feet like the gleam of polished bronze, and the sound of his words like the sound of a multitude.

Only I, Daniel, saw the vision. The men who were with me did not see it, but a great terror fell on them, and they ran and hid …

Suddenly, a hand touched me and set me shaking on my hands and knees. He said to me, "Daniel, you are a man treasured by God. Understand the words that I'm saying to you. Stand on your feet, for I have now been sent to you." After he said this to me, I stood trembling.

"Don't be afraid, Daniel," he said to me, "for from the first day that you purposed to understand and to humble yourself before your God, your prayers were heard. I have come because of your prayers.

—Daniel 10:4-7, 10-12 CSB

Big Idea #7

Humanity

Then the rib which the Lord God had taken from man He made into a woman, and He brought her to the man. And Adam said: "This is now bone of my bones And flesh of my flesh; She shall be called Woman, Because she was taken out of Man." Therefore a man shall leave his father and mother and be joined to his wife, and they shall become one flesh.

—Genesis 2:22-24 NKJV

\\\

When God created humankind, he made them in the likeness of God. Male and female he created them, and he blessed them and named them "Humankind" when they were created.

—Genesis 5:1-2 NRSV

///

The Lord said to Himself, "I will never again curse the ground on account of man, for the intent of man's heart is evil from his youth; and I will never again destroy every living thing, as I have done.

—Genesis 8:21 NASB

\\\

But the Lord said to Samuel, "Don't be impressed by his appearance or his height, for I have rejected him. God does not view things the way men do. People look on the outward appearance, but the Lord looks at the heart."

—1 Samuel 16:7 NET

///

What are human beings, that you make so much of them, that you set your mind on them, visit them every morning, test them every moment?

—Job 7:17-18 NRSV

\\\

The Spirit of God has made me, and the breath of the Almighty gives me life.

—Job 33:4 CSB

///

If God were to take back his spirit and withdraw his breath, all life would cease, and humanity would turn again to dust.

—Job 34:14-15 NLT

\\\

But why are people even important to you? Why do you take care of human beings? You made them a little lower than the angels and crowned them with glory and honor. You put them in charge of everything you made. You put all things under their control: all the sheep, the cattle, and the wild animals. the birds in the sky, the fish in the sea, and everything that lives under water.

—Psalm 8:4-8 NCV

///

The Lord looks down from heaven; he observes everyone … He forms the hearts of them all; he considers all their works.

—Psalm 33:13, 15 CSB

\\\

Lord, remind me how brief my time on earth will be. Remind me that my days are numbered—how fleeting my life is. You have made my life no longer than the width of my hand. My entire lifetime is just a moment to you; at best, each of us is but a breath. *Interlude*

We are merely moving shadows, and all our busy rushing ends in nothing. We heap up wealth, not knowing who will spend it. And so, Lord, where do I put my hope? My only hope is in you.

—Psalm 39:4-7 NLT

///

People, despite their wealth, do not endure; they are like the beasts that perish.

—Psalm 49:12 NIV

\\\

People are like a breath; their lives are like passing shadows.

—Psalm 144:4 NCV

///

A man who finds a wife finds a good thing and obtains favor from the Lord.

—Proverbs 18:22 CSB

\\\

The rich and poor meet together:
the Lord is the maker of them all.

—Proverbs 22:2 KJV

///

Don't brag about tomorrow, since you don't know what the day will bring.

—Proverbs 27:1 NLT

\\\

He has made everything beautiful in its time. Also He has put eternity in their hearts, except that no one can find out the work that God does from beginning to end.

—Ecclesiastes 3:11 NKJV

///

I said in my heart with regard to the children of man that God is testing them that they may see that they themselves are but beasts. For what happens to the children of man and what happens to the beasts is the same; as one dies, so dies the other. They all have the same breath, and man has no advantage over the beasts, for all is vanity. All go to one place. All are from the dust, and to dust all return.

—Ecclesiastes 3:18-20 ESV

\\\

For no one can anticipate the time of disaster. Like fish taken in a cruel net, and like birds caught in a snare, so mortals are snared at a time of calamity, when it suddenly falls upon them.

—Ecclesiastes 9:12 NRSV

///

Don't put your trust in mere humans. They are as frail as breath. What good are they?

—Isaiah 2:22 NLT

\\\

Lord, we know that people do not control their own destiny. It is not in their power to determine what will happen to them.

—Jeremiah 10:23 NET

///

The person who sins shall die. A child shall not suffer for the iniquity of a parent, nor a parent suffer for the iniquity of a child; the righteousness of the righteous shall be his own, and the wickedness of the wicked shall be his own.

—Ezekiel 18:20 NRSV

Big Idea #8

The Sin Problem

Now the serpent was the most cunning of all the wild animals that the Lord God had made. He said to the woman, "Did God really say, 'You can't eat from any tree in the garden'?"

The woman said to the serpent, "We may eat the fruit from the trees in the garden. But about the fruit of the tree in the middle of the garden, God said, 'You must not eat it or touch it, or you will die.'"

"No! You will not die," the serpent said to the woman. "In fact, God knows that when you eat it your eyes will be opened and you will be like God, knowing good and evil." The woman saw that the tree was good for food and delightful to look at, and that it was desirable for obtaining wisdom. So she took some of its fruit and ate it; she also gave some to her husband, who was with her, and he ate it. …

So the Lord God asked the woman, "What is this you have done?"

And the woman said, "The serpent deceived me, and I ate."

—Genesis 3:1-6, 13 CSB

\\\

The Lord saw that the wickedness of humankind was great in the earth, and that every inclination of the thoughts of their hearts was only evil continually

—Genesis 6:5 NRSV

///

If a person sins and does something the Lord has commanded not to be done, even if he does not know it, he is still guilty. He is responsible for his sin.

—Leviticus 5:17 NCV

\\\

Be sure your sin will find you out.

—Numbers 32:23 NRSV

///

Then the Spirit of God came on Zechariah son of Jehoiada the priest. He stood before the people and said, "This is what God says: 'Why do you disobey the Lord's commands? You will not prosper. Because you have forsaken the Lord, he has forsaken you.'"

—2 Chronicles 24:20 NIV

\\\

And I said:

My God, I am ashamed and embarrassed to lift my face toward you, my God, because our iniquities are higher than our heads and our guilt is as high as the heavens.

—Ezra 9:6 CSB

///

O God, you take no pleasure in wickedness; you cannot tolerate the sins of the wicked. Therefore, the proud may not stand in your presence, for you hate all who do evil. You will destroy those who tell lies. The Lord detests murderers and deceivers.

—Psalm 5:4-6 NLT

\\\

In arrogance the wicked hotly pursue the poor; let them be caught in the schemes that they have devised. For the wicked boasts of the desires of his soul, and the one greedy for gain curses and renounces the Lord.

In the pride of his face the wicked does not seek him; all his thoughts are, "There is no God." His ways prosper at all times; your judgments are on high, out of his sight; as for all his foes, he puffs at them. He says in his heart, "I shall not be moved; throughout all generations I shall not meet adversity."

His mouth is filled with cursing and deceit and oppression; under his tongue are mischief and iniquity. He sits in ambush in the villages; in hiding places he murders the innocent. His eyes stealthily watch for the helpless; he lurks in ambush like a lion in his thicket; he lurks that he may seize the poor; he seizes the poor when he draws him into his net.

The helpless are crushed, sink down, and fall by his might. He says in his heart, "God has forgotten, he has hidden his face, he will never see it."

—Psalm 10:2-11 ESV

///

The fool has said in his heart, "There is no God." They are corrupt, They have done abominable works, There is none who does good.

The Lord looks down from heaven upon the children of men, To see if there are any who understand, who seek God.

They have all turned aside, They have together become corrupt; There is none who does good, No, not one.

—Psalm 14:1-3 NKJV

\\\

Indeed, I was guilty when I was born;
I was sinful when my mother conceived me.

—Psalm 51:5 CSB

///

From birth, evil people turn away from God; they wander off and tell lies as soon as they are born.

—Psalm 58:3 NCV

\\\

The way of the wicked is as darkness: they know not at what they stumble.

—Proverbs 4:19 KJV

///

An evil man will be caught in his wicked ways; the ropes of his sins will tie him up.

—Proverbs 5:22 NCV

\\\

The wicked is snared by the transgression of his lips: but the just shall come out of trouble.

—Proverbs 12:13 KJV

///

Who can say, I have made my heart clean, I am pure from my sin?

—Proverbs 20:9 KJV

\\\

Not a single person on earth is always good and never sins.

—Ecclesiastes 7:20 NLT

///

The hearts of all people are full of evil, and there is folly in their hearts during their lives—then they die.

—Ecclesiastes 9:3 NET

\\\

But your sinful acts have alienated you from your God; your sins have caused him to reject you and not listen to your prayers.

—Isaiah 59:2 NET

///

But we are all as an unclean thing, and all our righteousnesses are as filthy rags; and we all do fade as a leaf; and our iniquities, like the wind, have taken us away.

—Isaiah 64:6 KJV

\\\

Can an Ethiopian change his skin or a leopard its spots? Neither can you do good who are accustomed to doing evil.

—Jeremiah 13:23 NIV

///

Therefore say to the people of Israel, 'This is what the Sovereign Lord says: Repent! Turn from your idols and renounce all your detestable practices!

—Ezekiel 14:6 NIV

Big Idea #9

Evil and Suffering

So the Lord God asked the woman, "What is this you have done?"

And the woman said, "The serpent deceived me, and I ate." … He said to the woman: I will intensify your labor pains; you will bear children with painful effort. Your desire will be for your husband, yet he will rule over you …

And he said to the man, "Because you listened to your wife and ate from the tree about which I commanded you, 'Do not eat from it': The ground is cursed because of you. You will eat from it by means of painful labor all the days of your life. It will produce thorns and thistles for you, and you will eat the plants of the field. You will eat bread by the sweat of your brow until you return to the ground, since you were taken from it. For you are dust, and you will return to dust."

—Genesis 3:13, 16-19 CSB

\\\

Our ancestors were unfaithful to God and did what the Lord said was wrong. They left the Lord and stopped worshiping at the Temple where he lives. They rejected him.

—2 Chronicles 29:6 NCV

///

As I have observed, those who plow evil and those who sow trouble reap it.

—Job 4:8 NIV

\\\

How long, O Lord? Will You forget me forever? How long will You hide Your face from me? How long shall I take counsel in my soul, Having sorrow in my heart all the day? How long will my enemy be exalted over me?

—Psalm 13:1-2 NASB

///

My God, my God, why have you forsaken me? Why are you so far from helping me, from the words of my groaning? O my God, I cry by day, but you do not answer; and by night, but find no rest.

—Psalm 22:1-2 NRSV

\\\

Sin speaks to the wicked in their hearts. They have no fear of God. They think too much of themselves so they don't see their sin and hate it. Their words are wicked lies; they are no longer wise or good. At night they make evil plans; what they do leads to nothing good. They don't refuse things that are evil.

—Psalm 36:1-4 NCV

///

My whole body is sick because of your judgment; I am deprived of health because of my sin. For my sins overwhelm me; like a heavy load, they are too much for me to bear.

—Psalm 38:3-4 NET

\\\

But as for me, my feet almost slipped; my steps nearly went astray. For I envied the arrogant; I saw the prosperity of the wicked.

They have an easy time until they die, and their bodies are well fed. They are not in trouble like others; they are not afflicted like most people. Therefore, pride is their necklace, and violence covers them like a garment. Their eyes bulge out from fatness; the imaginations of their hearts run wild. They mock, and they speak maliciously; they arrogantly threaten oppression. They set their mouths against heaven, and their tongues strut across the earth. Therefore his people turn to them and drink in their overflowing words. The wicked say, "How can God know? Does the Most High know everything?" Look at them—the wicked! They are always at ease, and they increase their wealth.

Did I purify my heart and wash my hands in innocence for nothing? For I am afflicted all day long and punished every morning. If I had decided to say these things aloud, I would have betrayed your people. When I tried to understand all this, it seemed hopeless until I entered God's sanctuary. Then I understood their destiny. Indeed, you put them in slippery places; you make them fall into ruin. How suddenly they become a desolation! They come to an end, swept away by terrors.

—Psalm 73:2-19 CSB

///

It was good for me to suffer so I would learn your demands.

—Psalm 119:71 NCV

\\\

These men lie in wait for their own blood; they ambush only themselves! Such are the paths of all who go after ill-gotten gain; it takes away the life of those who get it.

—Proverbs 1:18-19 NIV

///

For they hated knowledge and chose not to fear the Lord. They rejected my advice and paid no attention when I corrected them. Therefore, they must eat the bitter fruit of living their own way, choking on their own schemes.

—Proverbs 1:29-31 NLT

\\\

An evil man will be caught in his wicked ways; the ropes of his sins will tie him up. He will die because he does not control himself, and he will be held captive by his foolishness.

—Proverbs 5:22-23 NCV

///

The fear of the Lord is to hate evil; I hate arrogant pride and the evil way and perverse utterances.

—Proverbs 8:13 NET

\\\

Genuine righteousness leads to life, but pursuing evil leads to death.

—Proverbs 11:19 CSB

///

Whoever sows injustice reaps calamity, and the rod they wield in fury will be broken.

—Proverbs 22:8 NIV

\\\

What sorrow for those who say that evil is good and good is evil, that dark is light and light is dark, that bitter is sweet and sweet is bitter.

—Isaiah 5:20 NLT

///

For a fool speaks foolishness and his mind plots iniquity. He lives in a godless way and speaks falsely about the Lord. He leaves the hungry empty and deprives the thirsty of drink.

—Isaiah 32:6 CSB

\\\

"But those who still reject me are like the restless sea, which is never still but continually churns up mud and dirt. There is no peace for the wicked," says my God.

—Isaiah 57:20-21 NLT

Big Idea #10

God's Solution

Abraham is to become a great and powerful nation, and all the nations of the earth will be blessed through him.

—Genesis 18:18 CSB

\\\

But from there you will seek the Lord your God, and you will find Him if you search for Him with all your heart and all your soul.

—Deuteronomy 4:29 NASB

///

Moses continued, "The Lord your God will raise up for you a prophet like me from among your fellow Israelites. You must listen to him."

—Deuteronomy 18:15 NLT

\\\

For if you return to the Lord, your brothers and your children will find compassion with their captors and return to this land. For the Lord your God is gracious and merciful and will not turn away his face from you, if you return to him.

—2 Chronicles 30:9 ESV

///

As for me, I know that my Redeemer lives, And at the last He will take His stand on the earth.

—Job 19:25 NASB

\\\

But I have trusted in Your lovingkindness; My heart shall rejoice in Your salvation.

—Psalm 13:5 NASB

///

Happy is the person whose sins are forgiven, whose wrongs are pardoned. Happy is the person whom the Lord does not consider guilty and in whom there is nothing false.

—Psalm 32:1-2 NCV

\\\

I said, "Lord, be gracious to me; heal me, for I have sinned against you."

—Psalm 41:4 CSB

///

Have mercy on me, O God, according to your steadfast love; according to your abundant mercy blot out my transgressions. Wash me thoroughly from my iniquity, and cleanse me from my sin.

—Psalm 51:1-2 NRSV

\\\

Create in me a clean heart, O God, and put a new and right spirit within me … Deliver me from bloodshed, O God, O God of my salvation, and my tongue will sing aloud of your deliverance.

—Psalm 51:10, 14 NRSV

///

Blessed be the Lord! Day after day he bears our burdens;
God is our salvation.
Selah
Our God is a God of salvation, and escape from death belongs to the Lord my Lord.

—Psalm 68:19-20 CSB

\\\

For You, Lord, are good, and ready to forgive,
And abundant in mercy to all those who call upon You.

—Psalm 86:5 NKJV

///

He provided redemption for his people; he ordained his covenant forever—holy and awesome is his name.

—Psalm 111:9 NIV

\\\

People who conceal their sins will not prosper, but if they confess and turn from them, they will receive mercy.

—Proverbs 28:13 NLT

///

"Come now, and let us reason together," Says the Lord, "Though your sins are like scarlet, They shall be as white as snow; Though they are red like crimson, They shall be as wool.

—Isaiah 1:18 NKJV

\\\

For unto us a child is born, unto us a son is given: and the government shall be upon his shoulder: and his name shall be called Wonderful, Counsellor, The mighty God, The everlasting Father, The Prince of Peace.

—Isaiah 9:6 KJV

///

He will destroy death forever. The Lord God will wipe away the tears from every face and remove his people's disgrace from the whole earth, for the Lord has spoken.

On that day it will be said, "Look, this is our God; we have waited for him, and he has saved us. This is the Lord; we have waited for him. Let us rejoice and be glad in his salvation."

—Isaiah 25:8-9 CSB

\\\

Turn to me and be saved, all the ends of the earth! For I am God, and there is no other.

—Isaiah 45:22 ESV

///

Surely he hath borne our griefs, and carried our sorrows: yet we did esteem him stricken, smitten of God, and afflicted. But he was wounded for our transgressions, he was bruised for our iniquities: the chastisement of our peace was upon him; and with his stripes we are healed. All we like sheep have gone astray; we have turned every one to his own way; and the Lord hath laid on him the iniquity of us all.

—Isaiah 53:4-6 KJV

\\\

Yet it was the Lord's will to crush him and cause him to suffer, and though the Lord makes his life an offering for sin, he will see his offspring and prolong his days, and the will of the Lord will prosper in his hand …

Therefore I will give him a portion among the great, and he will divide the spoils with the strong, because he poured out his life unto death, and was numbered with the transgressors. For he bore the sin of many, and made intercession for the transgressors.

—Isaiah 53:10, 12 NIV

///

Come, everyone who thirsts, come to the waters; and he who has no money, come, buy and eat! Come, buy wine and milk without money and without price.

Why do you spend your money for that which is not bread, and your labor for that which does not satisfy? Listen diligently to me, and eat what is good, and delight yourselves in rich food. Incline your ear, and come to me; hear, that your soul may live; and I will make with you an everlasting covenant, my steadfast, sure love for David.

—Isaiah 55:1-3 ESV

\\\

Seek the Lord while he may be found; call on him while he is near. Let the wicked forsake their ways and the unrighteous their thoughts. Let them turn to the Lord, and he will have mercy on them, and to our God, for he will freely pardon.

—Isaiah 55:6-7 NIV

///

And I will give them an heart to know me, that I am the Lord: and they shall be my people, and I will be their God: for they shall return unto me with their whole heart.

—Jeremiah 24:7 KJV

\\\

The days are surely coming, says the Lord, when I will make a new covenant with the house of Israel and the house of Judah. It will not be like the covenant that I made with their ancestors when I took them by the hand to bring them out of the land of Egypt—a covenant that they broke, though I was their husband, says the Lord. But this is the covenant that I will make with the house of Israel after those days, says the Lord: I will put my law within them, and I will write it on their hearts; and I will be their God, and they shall be my people. No longer shall they teach one another, or say to each other, "Know the Lord," for they shall all know me, from the least of them to the greatest, says the Lord; for I will forgive their iniquity, and remember their sin no more.

—Jeremiah 31:31-34 NRSV

///

And I will make an everlasting covenant with them, that I will not turn away from them, to do them good; but I will put my fear in their hearts, that they shall not depart from me.

—Jeremiah 32:40 KJV

\\\

Say to them: 'As I live,' says the Lord God, 'I have no pleasure in the death of the wicked, but that the wicked turn from his way and live. Turn, turn from your evil ways! For why should you die, O house of Israel?'

—Ezekiel 33:11 NKJV

///

I will ransom them from the power of the grave; I will redeem them from death. O Death, I will be your plagues! O Grave, I will be your destruction!

—Hosea 13:14 NKJV

\\\

Yet even now, says the Lord, return to me with all your heart, with fasting, with weeping, and with mourning; rend your hearts and not your clothing.

Return to the Lord, your God, for he is gracious and merciful, slow to anger, and abounding in steadfast love, and relents from punishing.

—Joel 2:12-13 NRSV

///

Therefore I will look unto the Lord; I will wait for the God of my salvation: my God will hear me.

—Micah 7:7 KJV

\\\

And the Lord their God shall save them in that day as the flock of his people: for they shall be as the stones of a crown, lifted up as an ensign upon his land.

—Zechariah 9:16 KJV

Big Idea #11

Becoming Holy

But from there you will seek the Lord your God, and you will find Him if you search for Him with all your heart and all your soul.

—Deuteronomy 4:29 NASB

\\\

Know then in your heart that as a parent disciplines a child so the Lord your God disciplines you.

—Deuteronomy 8:5 NRSV

///

Love the Lord your God and keep his requirements, his decrees, his laws and his commands always … Faithfully obey the commands I am giving you today—to love the Lord your God and to serve him with all your heart and with all your soul.

—Deuteronomy 11:1, 13 NIV

\\\

I call heaven and earth as witnesses against you today that I have set before you life and death, blessing and curse. Choose life so that you and your descendants may live, 20 love the Lord your God, obey him, and remain faithful to him. For he is your life, and he will prolong your days as you live in the land the Lord swore to give to your fathers Abraham, Isaac, and Jacob.

—Deuteronomy 30:19-20 CSB

///

This book of the law shall not depart from your mouth, but you shall meditate on it day and night, so that you may be careful to do according to all that is written in it; for then you will make your way prosperous, and then you will have success.

—Joshua 1:8 NASB

\\\

Because your heart was responsive and you humbled yourself before the Lord when you heard what I have spoken against this place and its people—that they would become a curse and be laid waste—and because you tore your robes and wept in my presence, I also have heard you, declares the Lord.

—2 Kings 22:19 NIV

///

Seek the Lord and his strength, seek his face continually.

—1 Chronicles 16:11 KJV

\\\

But consider the joy of those corrected by God! Do not despise the discipline of the Almighty when you sin. For though he wounds, he also bandages. He strikes, but his hands also heal.

—Job 5:17-18 NLT

///

You have granted me life and lovingkindness; And Your care has preserved my spirit.

—Job 10:12 NASB

\\\

Blessed is the man
Who walks not in the counsel of the ungodly,
Nor stands in the path of sinners,
Nor sits in the seat of the scornful;
But his delight is in the law of the Lord,
And in His law he meditates day and night.

—Psalm 1:1-2 NKJV

///

The Lord is my shepherd; I shall not want. He maketh me to lie down in green pastures: he leadeth me beside the still waters. He restoreth my soul: he leadeth me in the paths of righteousness for his name's sake.

—Psalm 23:1-3 KJV

\\\

Show me Your ways, O Lord; Teach me Your paths. Lead me in Your truth and teach me, For You are the God of my salvation; On You I wait all the day.

—Psalm 25:4-5 NKJV

///

My heart says this about you: “Seek his face.” Lord, I will seek your face.

—Psalm 27:8 CSB

\\\

The sacrifice pleasing to God is a broken spirit. You will not despise a broken and humbled heart, God.

—Psalm 51:17 CSB

///

I will remember the Lord’s works; yes, I will remember your ancient wonders. I will reflect on all you have done and meditate on your actions.

—Psalm 77:11-12 CSB

\\\

My child, if sinners try to lead you into sin, do not follow them.

—Proverbs 1:10 NCV

My child, do not reject the Lord’s discipline, and don’t get angry when he corrects you. The Lord corrects those he loves, just as parents correct the child they delight in.

—Proverbs 3:11-12 NCV

///

The highway of the upright avoids evil; those who guard their way preserve their lives.

—Proverbs 16:17 NRSV

\\\

Even the youths shall faint and be weary, and the young men shall utterly fall: But they that wait upon the Lord shall renew their strength; they shall mount up with wings as eagles; they shall run, and not be weary; and they shall walk, and not faint.

—Isaiah 40:30-31 KJV

///

For the High and Exalted One, who lives forever, whose name is holy, says this: "I live in a high and holy place, and with the oppressed and lowly of spirit, to revive the spirit of the lowly and revive the heart of the oppressed.

—Isaiah 57:15 CSB

\\\

And I will give them an heart to know me, that I am the Lord: and they shall be my people, and I will be their God: for they shall return unto me with their whole heart.

—Jeremiah 24:7 KJV

///

The Lord is good to those who wait for him, to the soul that seeks him. It is good that one should wait quietly for the salvation of the Lord.

—Lamentations 3:25-26 NRSV

\\\

Then I will sprinkle clean water on you, and you shall be clean; I will cleanse you from all your filthiness and from all your idols. I will give you a new heart and put a new spirit within you; I will take the heart of stone out of your flesh and give you a heart of flesh. I will put My Spirit within you and cause you to walk in My statutes, and you will keep My judgments and do them. Then you shall dwell in the land that I gave to your fathers; you shall be My people, and I will be your God.

—Ezekiel 36:25-28 NKJV

///

Sow righteousness for yourselves, reap unfailing love. Break up the unplowed ground for yourselves, for it is time to seek the Lord, until he comes and showers deliverance on you.

—Hosea 10:12 NET

Big Idea #12

Living Faith

Then God gave the people all these instructions:

"I am the Lord your God, who rescued you from the land of Egypt, the place of your slavery.

"You must not have any other god but me.

"You must not make for yourself an idol of any kind or an image of anything in the heavens or on the earth or in the sea. You must not bow down to them or worship them, for I, the Lord your God, am a jealous God who will not tolerate your affection for any other gods. I lay the sins of the parents upon their children; the entire family is affected—even children in the third and fourth generations of those who reject me. But I lavish unfailing love for a thousand generations on those who love me and obey my commands.

"You must not misuse the name of the Lord your God. The Lord will not let you go unpunished if you misuse his name.

"Remember to observe the Sabbath day by keeping it holy. You have six days each week for your ordinary work, but the seventh day is a Sabbath day of rest dedicated to the Lord your God. On that day no one in your household may do any work. This includes you, your sons and daughters, your male and female servants, your livestock, and any foreigners living among you. For in six days the Lord made the heavens, the earth, the sea, and everything in them; but on the seventh day he rested. That is why the Lord blessed the Sabbath day and set it apart as holy.

"Honor your father and mother. Then you will live a long, full life in the land the Lord your God is giving you.

"You must not murder.

"You must not commit adultery.

"You must not steal.

"You must not testify falsely against your neighbor.

"You must not covet your neighbor's house. You must not covet your neighbor's wife, male or female servant, ox or donkey, or anything else that belongs to your neighbor."

—Exodus 20:1-17 NLT

\\\

Do not take revenge or bear a grudge against members of your community, but love your neighbor as yourself; I am the Lord.

—Leviticus 19:18 CSB

///

Stand up in the presence of the elderly, and show respect for the aged. Fear your God. I am the Lord.

—Leviticus 19:32 NLT

\\\

Love the Lord your God with all your heart, with all your soul, and with all your strength.

—Deuteronomy 6:5 CSB

///

Now, Israel, what does the Lord your God require from you, but to fear the Lord your God, to walk in all His ways and love Him, and to serve the Lord your God with all your heart and with all your soul, and to keep the Lord's commandments and His statutes which I am commanding you today for your good?

—Deuteronomy 10:12-13 NASB

\\\

But Samuel replied, "What is more pleasing to the Lord: your burnt offerings and sacrifices or your obedience to his voice? Listen! Obedience is better than sacrifice, and submission is better than offering the fat of rams."

—1 Samuel 15:22 NLT

///

Yea, though I walk through the valley of the shadow of death, I will fear no evil; For You are with me; Your rod and Your staff, they comfort me.

—Psalm 23:4 NKJV

\\\

I remain confident of this: I will see the goodness of the Lord in the land of the living. Wait for the Lord; be strong and take heart and wait for the Lord.

—Psalm 27:13-14 NIV

///

Delight yourself in the Lord, and he will give you the desires of your heart. Commit your way to the Lord; trust in him, and he will act. He will bring forth your righteousness as the light, and your justice as the noonday.

—Psalm 37:4-6 ESV

\\\

A good man deals graciously and lends;
He will guide his affairs with discretion.

—Psalm 112:5 NKJV

///

I lift up my eyes to the hills—from where will my help come? My help comes from the Lord, who made heaven and earth.
He will not let your foot be moved; he who keeps you will not slumber.

—Psalm 121:1-3 NRSV

\\\

Search me, God, and know my heart; test me and know my concerns. See if there is any offensive way in me; lead me in the everlasting way.

—Psalm 139:23-24 CSB

///

Teach me to do Your will, For You are my God; Let Your good Spirit lead me on level ground.

—Psalm 143:10 NASB

\\\

Trust in the Lord with all your heart, And lean not on your own understanding; In all your ways acknowledge Him, And He shall direct your paths.

—Proverbs 3:5-6 NKJV

///

Honor the Lord with your possessions and with the first produce of your entire harvest; then your barns will be completely filled, and your vats will overflow with new wine.

—Proverbs 3:9-10 CSB

\\\

Be careful what you think, because your thoughts run your life.

—Proverbs 4:23 NCV

///

Let your fountain be blessed, and rejoice in the wife of your youth, a lovely deer, a graceful doe. Let her breasts fill you at all times with delight; be intoxicated always in her love.

—Proverbs 5:18-19 ESV

\\\

It is a sin to belittle one's neighbor;
blessed are those who help the poor.

—Proverbs 14:21 NLT

///

Train up a child in the way he should go: and when he is old, he will not depart from it.

—Proverbs 22:6 KJV

\\\

Listen to your father who gave you life, and do not despise your mother when she is old.

—Proverbs 23:22 ESV

///

If your enemy is hungry, give him food to eat, and if he is thirsty, give him water to drink.

—Proverbs 25:21 NET

\\\

Charm is deceitful, and beauty is vain, but a woman who fears the Lord is to be praised.

—Proverbs 31:30 KJV

///

Let us hear the conclusion of the whole matter: Fear God, and keep his commandments: for this is the whole duty of man.

—Ecclesiastes 12:13 KJV

\\\

These are the ones I look on with favor: those who are humble and contrite in spirit, and who tremble at my word

—Isaiah 66:2 NIV

///

He has shown you, O man, what is good; And what does the Lord require of you But to do justly, To love mercy, And to walk humbly with your God?

—Micah 6:8 NKJV

\\\

This is what the Lord of Heaven's Armies says: Judge fairly, and show mercy and kindness to one another. Do not oppress widows, orphans, foreigners, and the poor. And do not scheme against each other.

—Zechariah 7:9-10 NLT

///

Bring the whole tithe into the storehouse, that there may be food in my house. Test me in this," says the Lord Almighty, "and see if I will not throw open the floodgates of heaven and pour out so much blessing that there will not be room enough to store it.

—Malachi 3:10 NIV

Big Idea #13

Wisdom

Wisdom is found with the elderly, and understanding comes with long life.

—Job 12:12 CSB

\\\

The counsel of the Lord stands forever, the plans of his heart from generation to generation.

—Psalm 33:11 CSB

///

So teach us to number our days, that we may apply our hearts unto wisdom.

—Psalm 90:12 KJV

Who is wise? Let him give heed to these things, And consider the lovingkindnesses of the Lord.

—Psalm 107:43 NASB

\\\

The fear of the Lord is the beginning of wisdom; all those who practice it have a good understanding. His praise endures forever.

—Psalm 111:10 NRSV

///

Teach me good judgment and knowledge, for I believe in your commandments.

—Psalm 119:66 NRSV

\\\

For the Lord gives wisdom; from his mouth come knowledge and understanding.

—Proverbs 2:6 CSB

///

Blessed is the one who finds wisdom, and the one who obtains understanding.

—Proverbs 3:13 NET

\\\

Pride leads only to shame; it is wise to be humble.

—Proverbs 11:2 NCV

///

Whoever walks with the wise becomes wise, but the companion of fools will suffer harm.

—Proverbs 13:20 ESV

\\\

Every wise woman builds her household, but a foolish woman tears it down with her own hands.

—Proverbs 14:1 NET

///

Get wisdom—how much better it is than gold! And get understanding—it is preferable to silver.

—Proverbs 16:16 CSB

\\\

Even a fool who keeps silent is considered wise; when he closes his lips, he is deemed intelligent.

—Proverbs 17:28 ESV

///

He who gets wisdom loves his own soul; He who keeps understanding will find good.

—Proverbs 19:8 NKJV

\\\

Listen, my son, and be wise, and set your heart on the right path: Do not join those who drink too much wine or gorge themselves on meat, for drunkards and gluttons become poor, and drowsiness clothes them in rags.

—Proverbs 23:19-21 NIV

///

Trusting unfaithful people when you are in trouble is like eating with a broken tooth or walking with a crippled foot.

—Proverbs 25:19 NCV

\\\

For to the one who pleases him, God gives wisdom, knowledge, and joy.

—Ecclesiastes 2:26 NET

///

Do not say, "Why were the old days better than these days?" for it is not wise to ask that.

—Ecclesiastes 7:10 NET

\\\

For wisdom is protection just as money is protection, But the advantage of knowledge is that wisdom preserves the lives of its possessors.

—Ecclesiastes 7:12 NASB

///

Who is a wise person? Who knows the solution to a problem? A person's wisdom brightens his appearance, and softens his harsh countenance.

—Ecclesiastes 8:1 NET

\\\

The words of a wise man's mouth are gracious; but the lips of a fool will swallow up himself.

—Ecclesiastes 10:12 KJV

Big Idea #14

Worship

Miriam the prophetess, the sister of Aaron, took a hand-drum in her hand, and all the women went out after her with hand-drums and with dances. Miriam sang in response to them, "Sing to the Lord, for he has triumphed gloriously; the horse and its rider he has thrown into the sea."

—Exodus 15:20-21 NET

\\\

Therefore I will give thanks to You, O Lord, among the nations,
And I will sing praises to Your name.

—2 Samuel 22:50 NASB

///

Give thanks unto the Lord, call upon his name, make known his deeds among the people.

—1 Chronicles 16:8 KJV

\\\

They are to stand every morning to thank and to praise the Lord, and likewise at evening.

—1 Chronicles 23:30 NASB

///

Then David blessed the Lord in the presence of all the assembly; David said: "Blessed are you, O Lord, the God of our ancestor Israel, forever and ever. Yours, O Lord, are the greatness, the power, the glory, the victory, and the majesty; for all that is in the heavens and on the earth is yours; yours is the kingdom, O Lord, and you are exalted as head above all. Riches and honor come from you, and you rule over all. In your hand are power and might; and it is in your hand to make great and to give strength to all. And now, our God, we give thanks to you and praise your glorious name.

—1 Chronicles 29:10-13 NRSV

\\\

The trumpeters and singers joined together to praise and thank the Lord with one voice. They raised their voices, accompanied by trumpets, cymbals, and musical instruments, in praise to the Lord:

For he is good; his faithful love endures forever.

The temple, the Lord's temple, was filled with a cloud. And because of the cloud, the priests were not able to continue ministering, for the glory of the Lord filled God's temple.

—2 Chronicles 5:13-14 CSB

///

Jehoshaphat listened to the people's advice. Then he chose men to be singers to the Lord, to praise him because he is holy and wonderful.

As they marched in front of the army, they said, "Thank the Lord, because his love continues forever."

—2 Chronicles 20:21 NCV

\\\

Moreover Hezekiah the king and the princes commanded the Levites to sing praise unto the Lord with the words of David, and of Asaph the seer. And they sang praises with gladness, and they bowed their heads and worshipped.

—2 Chronicles 29:30 KJV

///

They sang, praising and giving thanks to the Lord, saying, "For He is good, for His lovingkindness is upon Israel forever." And all the people shouted with a great shout when they praised the Lord because the foundation of the house of the Lord was laid.

—Ezra 3:11 NASB

\\\

Ezra praised the Lord, the great God; and all the people lifted their hands and responded, "Amen! Amen!" Then they bowed down and worshiped the Lord with their faces to the ground.

—Nehemiah 8:6 NIV

///

Then Job arose, tore his robe, and shaved his head; and he fell to the ground and worshiped. And he said:

"Naked I came from my mother's womb, And naked shall I return there. The Lord gave, and the Lord has taken away; Blessed be the name of the Lord."

—Job 1:20-21 NKJV

\\\

O Lord, our Lord, your majestic name fills the earth! Your glory is higher than the heavens. You have taught children and infants to tell of your strength, silencing your enemies and all who oppose you …

O Lord, our Lord, your majestic name fills the earth!

—Psalm 8:1-2, 9 NLT

///

I will bless the Lord at all times; his praise shall continually be in my mouth. My soul makes its boast in the Lord; let the humble hear and be glad. Oh, magnify the Lord with me, and let us exalt his name together!

—Psalm 34:1-3 ESV

\\\

It is good to praise you, Lord, to sing praises to God Most High. It is good to tell of your love in the morning and of your loyalty at night. It is good to praise you with the ten-stringed lyre and with the soft-sounding harp. Lord, you have made me happy by what you have done; I will sing for joy about what your hands have done.

—Psalm 92:1-4 NCV

///

O come, let us sing unto the Lord: let us make a joyful noise to the rock of our salvation. Let us come before his presence with thanksgiving, and make a joyful noise unto him with psalms. For the Lord is a great God, and a great King above all gods …

O come, let us worship and bow down: let us kneel before the Lord our maker. For he is our God; and we are the people of his pasture, and the sheep of his hand.

—Psalm 95:1-3, 6-7 KJV

\\\

Make a joyful shout to the Lord, all you lands! Serve the Lord with gladness; Come before His presence with singing. Know that the Lord, He is God; It is He who has made us, and not we ourselves; We are His people and the sheep of His pasture.

Enter into His gates with thanksgiving, And into His courts with praise. Be thankful to Him, and bless His name.

—Psalm 100:1-4 NKJV

///

Bless the Lord, O my soul, and all that is within me, bless his holy name!

Bless the Lord, O my soul, and forget not all his benefits, who forgives all your iniquity, who heals all your diseases, who redeems your life from the pit, who crowns you with steadfast love and mercy, who satisfies you with good so that your youth is renewed like the eagle's.

—Psalm 103:1-5 ESV

\\\

I will exalt you, my God the King; I will praise your name for ever and ever. Every day I will praise you and extol your name for ever and ever. Great is the Lord and most worthy of praise; his greatness no one can fathom.

—Psalm 145:1-3 NIV

///

Hallelujah!

Praise the Lord from the heavens; praise him in the heights. Praise him, all his angels; praise him, all his heavenly armies. Praise him, sun and moon; praise him, all you shining stars. Praise him, highest heavens, and you waters above the heavens. Let them praise the name of the Lord, for he commanded, and they were created.

—Psalm 148:1-5 CSB

\\\

Praise ye the Lord. Praise God in his sanctuary: praise him in the firmament of his power.

Praise him for his mighty acts: praise him according to his excellent greatness.

Praise him with the sound of the trumpet: praise him with the psaltery and harp.

Praise him with the timbrel and dance: praise him with stringed instruments and organs.

Praise him upon the loud cymbals: praise him upon the high sounding cymbals.

Let every thing that hath breath praise the Lord. Praise ye the Lord.

—Psalm 150 KJV

///

Sing to the Lord, for he has done magnificent things, let this be known throughout the earth! Cry out and shout for joy, O citizens of Zion, for the Holy One of Israel acts mightily among you!

—Isaiah 12:5-6 NET

\\\

The Lord says: "These people worship me with their mouths, and honor me with their lips, but their hearts are far from me. Their worship is based on nothing but human rules.

—Isaiah 29:13 NCV

///

Sing, O heavens; and be joyful, O earth; and break forth into singing, O mountains: for the Lord hath comforted his people, and will have mercy upon his afflicted.

—Isaiah 49:13 KJV

\\\

Now I, Nebuchadnezzar, praise and extol and honor the King of heaven, for all his works are right and his ways are just; and those who walk in pride he is able to humble.

—Daniel 4:37 ESV

Big Idea #15

Prayer

The servant said, "Lord, God of my master Abraham, allow me to find a wife for his son today. Please show this kindness to my master Abraham. Here I am, standing by the spring, and the girls from the city are coming out to get water. I will say to one of them, 'Please put your jar down so I can drink.' Then let her say, 'Drink, and I will also give water to your camels.' If that happens, I will know she is the right one for your servant Isaac and that you have shown kindness to my master." Before the servant had finished praying, Rebekah, the daughter of Bethuel, came out of the city…

—Genesis 24:12-15 NCV

\\\

But from there you will seek the Lord your God, and you will find Him if you search for Him with all your heart and all your soul.

—Deuteronomy 4:29 NASB

///

Then Samson prayed to the Lord, "Lord God, remember me. God, please give me strength one more time so I can pay these Philistines back for putting out my two eyes!" Then Samson turned to the two center pillars that supported the whole temple. He braced himself between the two pillars, with his right hand on one and his left hand on the other. Samson said, "Let me die with these Philistines!" Then he pushed as hard as he could, causing the temple to fall on the rulers and all the people in it. So Samson killed more of the Philistines when he died than when he was alive.

—Judges 16:28-30 NCV

\\\

When Jacob went into Egypt, and the Egyptians oppressed them, then your fathers cried out to the Lord and the Lord sent Moses and Aaron, who brought your fathers out of Egypt and made them dwell in this place.

—1 Samuel 12:8 ESV

///

Moreover, as for me, far be it from me that I should sin against the Lord by ceasing to pray for you, and I will instruct you in the good and the right way.

—1 Samuel 12:23 ESV

\\\

Then Solomon stood before the altar of the Lord in front of the entire congregation of Israel and spread out his hands toward heaven.

He said:

Lord God of Israel, there is no God like you in heaven above or on earth below, who keeps the gracious covenant with your servants who walk before you with all their heart…

Listen to your servant's prayer and his petition, Lord my God, so that you may hear the cry and the prayer that your servant prays before you today, so that your eyes may watch over this temple night and day, toward the place where you said, "My name will be there," and so that you may hear the prayer that your servant prays toward this place.

Hear the petition of your servant and your people Israel, which they pray toward this place. May you hear in your dwelling place in heaven.

May you hear and forgive…

May your eyes be open to your servant's petition and to the petition of your people Israel, listening to them whenever they call to you.

—1 Kings 8:22-23, 28-30, 52 CSB

///

Jabez called upon the God of Israel, saying, "Oh that you would bless me and enlarge my border, and that your hand might be with me, and that you would keep me from harm so that it might not bring me pain!" And God granted what he asked.

—1 Chronicles 4:10 ESV

\\\

In his pain Manasseh asked the Lord his God for mercy and truly humbled himself before the God of his ancestors. When he prayed to the Lord, the Lord responded to him and answered favorably his cry for mercy. The Lord brought him back to Jerusalem to his kingdom. Then Manasseh realized that the Lord is the true God.

—2 Chronicles 33:12-13 NET

///

I proclaimed a fast by the Ahava River, so that we might humble ourselves before our God and ask him for a safe journey for us, our dependents, and all our possessions. I did this because I was ashamed to ask the king for infantry and cavalry to protect us from enemies during the journey, since we had told him, "The hand of our God is gracious to all who seek him, but his fierce anger is against all who abandon him." So we fasted and pleaded with our God about this, and he was receptive to our prayer.

—Ezra 8:21-23 CSB

\\\

I have set the Lord continually before me; Because He is at my right hand, I will not be shaken.

—Psalm 16:8 NASB

///

In my distress I called to the Lord; I cried out to my God. From his heavenly temple he heard my voice; he listened to my cry for help.

—Psalm 18:6 NET

\\\

Lord, hear my voice when I call; be gracious to me and answer me.

—Psalm 27:7 CSB

///

I waited patiently for the Lord; And He inclined to me, And heard my cry. He also brought me up out of a horrible pit, Out of the miry clay, And set my feet upon a rock, And established my steps. He has put a new song in my mouth—Praise to our God;

Many will see it and fear, And will trust in the Lord.

—Psalm 40:1-3 NKJV

\\\

Rest in God alone, my soul, for my hope comes from him. He alone is my rock and my salvation, my stronghold; I will not be shaken. My salvation and glory depend on God, my strong rock. My refuge is in God. Trust in him at all times, you people; pour out your hearts before him. God is our refuge.

—Psalm 62:5-8 CSB

///

O God, You are my God; Early will I seek You; My soul thirsts for You; My flesh longs for You In a dry and thirsty land Where there is no water.

—Psalm 63:1 NKJV

\\\

When I remember You on my bed, I meditate on You in the night watches, For You have been my help, And in the shadow of Your wings I sing for joy. My soul clings to You; Your right hand upholds me.

—Psalm 63:6-8 NASB

///

I will cry out to God and call for help! I will cry out to God and he will pay attention to me. In my time of trouble I sought the Lord. I kept my hand raised in prayer throughout the night. I refused to be comforted. I said, "I will remember God while I groan; I will think about him while my strength leaves me." …

—Psalm 77:1-3 NET

\\\

Because he bends down to listen, I will pray as long as I have breath!

Death wrapped its ropes around me; the terrors of the grave overtook me. I saw only trouble and sorrow.

Then I called on the name of the Lord: "Please, Lord, save me!"

How kind the Lord is! How good he is! So merciful, this God of ours! The Lord protects those of childlike faith; I was facing death, and he saved me.

—Psalm 116:2-6 NLT

///

Pray for the peace of Jerusalem: they shall prosper that love thee.

—Psalm 122:6 KJV

\\\

The Lord is near to all who call on him, to all who call on him in truth.

—Psalm 145:18 ESV

///

Also, seek the peace and prosperity of the city to which I have carried you into exile. Pray to the Lord for it, because if it prospers, you too will prosper.

—Jeremiah 29:7 NIV

\\\

"We are all in agreement—we administrators, officials, high officers, advisers, and governors—that the king should make a law that will be strictly enforced. Give orders that for the next thirty days any person who prays to anyone, divine or human—except to you, Your Majesty—will be thrown into the den of lions. And now, Your Majesty, issue and sign this law so it cannot be changed, an official law of the Medes and Persians that cannot be revoked." So King Darius signed the law.

But when Daniel learned that the law had been signed, he went home and knelt down as usual in his upstairs room, with its windows open toward Jerusalem. He prayed three times a day, just as he had always done, giving thanks to his God. Then the officials went together to Daniel's house and found him praying and asking for God's help.

—Daniel 6:7-11 NLT

///

So I turned my attention to the Lord God to seek him by prayer and petitions, with fasting, sackcloth, and ashes.

I prayed to the Lord my God and confessed:

Ah, Lord—the great and awe-inspiring God who keeps his gracious covenant with those who love him and keep his commands—we have sinned, done wrong, acted wickedly, rebelled, and turned away from your commands and ordinances . . .

Listen closely, my God, and hear. Open your eyes and see our desolations and the city that bears your name. For we are not presenting our petitions before you based on our righteous acts, but based on your abundant compassion. Lord, hear! Lord, forgive! Lord, listen and act! My God, for your own sake, do not delay, because your city and your people bear your name.

—Daniel 9:3-5, 18-19 CSB

\\\

Come back to the Lord and say these words to him: "Take away all our sin and kindly receive us, and we will keep the promises we made to you."

—Hosea 14:2 NCV

Big Idea #16

The Bible

Then Moses turned and went down from the mountain with the two tablets of the testimony in his hand, tablets which were written on both sides; they were written on one side and the other. The tablets were God's work, and the writing was God's writing engraved on the tablets.

—Exodus 32:15-16 NASB

\\\

These words that I am giving you today are to be in your heart. Repeat them to your children. Talk about them when you sit in your house and when you walk along the road, when you lie down and when you get up. Bind them as a sign on your hand and let them be a symbol on your forehead. Write them on the doorposts of your house and on your city gates.

—Deuteronomy 6:6-9 CSB

///

When he becomes king, he should write a copy of the teachings on a scroll for himself, a copy taken from the priests and Levites. He should keep it with him all the time and read from it every day of his life. Then he will learn to respect the Lord his God, and he will obey all the teachings and commands. He should not think he is better than his fellow Israelites, and he must not stop obeying the law in any way so that he and his descendants may rule the kingdom for a long time.

—Deuteronomy 17:18-20 NCV

\\\

The secret things belong unto the Lord our God: but those things which are revealed belong unto us and to our children for ever, that we may do all the words of this law.

—Deuteronomy 29:29 KJV

///

When Moses had finished reciting all these words to all Israel, he said to them: "Take to heart all the words that I am giving in witness against you today; give them as a command to your children, so that they may diligently observe all the words of this law. This is no trifling matter for you, but rather your very life; through it you may live long in the land that you are crossing over the Jordan to possess."

—Deuteronomy 32:45-47 NRSV

\\\

This book of the law shall not depart from your mouth, but you shall meditate on it day and night, so that you may be careful to do according to all that is written in it; for then you will make your way prosperous, and then you will have success.

—Joshua 1:8 NASB

///

This God—his way is perfect; the word of the Lord proves true; he is a shield for all those who take refuge in him.

—2 Samuel 22:31 ESV

\\\

As for God, his way is perfect: The Lord's word is flawless; he shields all who take refuge in him.

—Psalm 18:30 NIV

///

The law of the Lord is perfect, reviving the soul; the testimony of the Lord is sure, making wise the simple; the precepts of the Lord are right, rejoicing the heart; the commandment of the Lord is pure, enlightening the eyes; the fear of the Lord is clean, enduring forever; the rules of the Lord are true, and righteous altogether. More to be desired are they than gold, even much fine gold; sweeter also than honey and drippings of the honeycomb. Moreover, by them is your servant warned; in keeping them there is great reward.

—Psalm 19:7-11 ESV

\\\

For the Lord's decrees are just, and everything he does is fair.

—Psalm 33:4 NET

///

Your word I have hidden in my heart, That I might not sin against You.

—Psalm 119:11 NKJV

\\\

Lord, your word is forever; it is firmly fixed in heaven. Your faithfulness is for all generations; you established the earth, and it stands firm. Your judgments stand firm today, for all things are your servants.

—Psalm 119:89-91 CSB

\\\

Your word is a lamp for my feet and a light on my path.

—Psalm 119:105 CSB

///

Establish my footsteps in Your word, And do not let any iniquity have dominion over me.

—Psalm 119:133 NASB

\\\

The sum of your word is truth, and every one of your righteous rules endures forever.

—Psalm 119:160 ESV

///

Every word of God is pure: he is a shield unto them that put their trust in him.

—Proverbs 30:5 KJV

///

A voice says, "Cry out." And I said, "What shall I cry?"

"All people are like grass, and all their faithfulness is like the flowers of the field. The grass withers and the flowers fall, because the breath of the Lord blows on them. Surely the people are grass. The grass withers and the flowers fall, but the word of our God endures forever."

—Isaiah 40:6-8 NIV

\\\

For as the rain comes down, and the snow from heaven,
And do not return there,
But water the earth,
And make it bring forth and bud,
That it may give seed to the sower And bread to the eater,
So shall My word be that goes forth from My mouth;
It shall not return to Me void,
But it shall accomplish what I please,
And it shall prosper in the thing for which I sent it.

—Isaiah 55:10-11 NKJV

Big Idea #17

Community of Faith

May God Almighty bless you and make you fruitful and multiply you so that you become an assembly of peoples.

—Genesis 28:3 CSB

\\\

Then he took the book of the covenant and read it in the hearing of the people; and they said, "All that the Lord has spoken we will do, and we will be obedient!"

—Exodus 24:7 NASB

///

Speak to the entire Israelite community and tell them: Be holy because I, the Lord your God, am holy.

—Leviticus 19:2 CSB

\\\

"Listen, Israel: The Lord our God, the Lord is one. Love the Lord your God with all your heart, with all your soul, and with all your strength. These words that I am giving you today are to be in your heart. Repeat them to your children. Talk about them when you sit in your house and when you walk along the road, when you lie down and when you get up. Bind them as a sign on your hand and let them be a symbol on your forehead. Write them on the doorposts of your house and on your city gates.

—Deuteronomy 6:4-9 CSB

///

For you are a people holy to the Lord your God. He has chosen you to be his people, prized above all others on the face of the earth.

—Deuteronomy 7:6 NET

\\\

You are holy people, who belong to the Lord your God. He has chosen you from all the people on earth to be his very own.

—Deuteronomy 14:2 NCV

///

At that time Joshua built an altar on Mount Ebal to the Lord, the God of Israel, just as Moses the Lord's servant had commanded the Israelites. He built it according to what is written in the book of the law of Moses: an altar of uncut stones on which no iron tool has been used. Then they offered burnt offerings to the Lord and sacrificed fellowship offerings on it. There on the stones, Joshua copied the law of Moses, which he had written in the presence of the Israelites. All Israel—resident alien and citizen alike—with their elders, officers, and judges, stood on either side of the ark of the Lord's covenant facing the Levitical priests who carried it. Half of them were in front of Mount Gerizim and half in front of Mount Ebal, as Moses the Lord's servant had commanded earlier concerning blessing the people of Israel. Afterward, Joshua read aloud all the words of the law—the blessings as well as the curses—according to all that is written in the book of the law. There was not a word of all that Moses had commanded that Joshua did not read before the entire assembly of Israel, including the women, the dependents, and the resident aliens who lived among them.

—Joshua 8:30-35 CSB

\\\

So the people came to Bethel and sat there before God until evening, and lifted up their voices and wept bitterly.

—Judges 21:2 NASB

///

The king summoned all the leaders of Judah and Jerusalem. The king went up to the Lord's temple, accompanied by all the people of Judah, all the residents of Jerusalem, the priests, and the prophets. All the people were there, from the youngest to the oldest. He read aloud all the words of the scroll of the covenant that had been discovered in the Lord's temple. The king stood by the pillar and renewed the covenant before the Lord, agreeing to follow the Lord and to obey his commandments, laws, and rules with all his heart and being, by carrying out the terms of this covenant recorded on this scroll. All the people agreed to keep the covenant.

—2 Kings 23:1-3 NET

\\\

If my people, which are called by my name, shall humble themselves, and pray, and seek my face, and turn from their wicked ways; then will I hear from heaven, and will forgive their sin, and will heal their land.

—2 Chronicles 7:14 KJV

///

Ezra praised the Lord, the great God; and all the people lifted their hands and responded, "Amen! Amen!" Then they bowed down and worshiped the Lord with their faces to the ground.

—Nehemiah 8:6 NIV

\\\

And they stood up in their place and read from the Book of the Law of the Lord their God for a quarter of the day; for another quarter of it they made confession and worshiped the Lord their God.

—Nehemiah 9:3 ESV

///

I will declare Your name to My brethren; In the midst of the assembly I will praise You.

—Psalm 22:22 NKJV

\\\

One thing have I desired of the Lord, that will I seek after; that I may dwell in the house of the Lord all the days of my life, to behold the beauty of the Lord, and to enquire in his temple.

—Psalm 27:4 KJV

///

I will give You thanks in the great congregation; I will praise You among a mighty throng.

—Psalm 35:18 NASB

\\\

People have seen your procession, God, the procession of my God, my King, in the sanctuary. Singers lead the way, with musicians following; among them are young women playing tambourines. Bless God in the assemblies; bless the Lord from the fountain of Israel.

—Psalm 68:24-26 CSB

///

Sing to the Lord, bless his name; tell of his salvation from day to day. Declare his glory among the nations, his marvelous works among all the peoples!

—Psalm 96:2-3 ESV

\\\

Enter into His gates with thanksgiving, And into His courts with praise. Be thankful to Him, and bless His name.

—Psalm 100:4 NKJV

///

I was glad when they said unto me,
Let us go into the house of the Lord.

—Psalm 122:1 KJV

\\\

How good and pleasant it is when brothers live together in harmony! It is like fine oil on the head, running down on the beard, running down Aaron's beard onto his robes. It is like the dew of Hermon falling on the mountains of Zion. For there the Lord has appointed the blessing—life forevermore.

—Psalm 133:1-3 CSB

///

Many peoples shall come and say, "Come, let us go up to the mountain of the Lord, to the house of the God of Jacob; that he may teach us his ways and that we may walk in his paths." For out of Zion shall go forth instruction, and the word of the Lord from Jerusalem.

—Isaiah 2:3 NRSV

Big Idea #18

Death and Eternity

The Lord God placed the man in the Garden of Eden to tend and watch over it. But the Lord God warned him, "You may freely eat the fruit of every tree in the garden—except the tree of the knowledge of good and evil. If you eat its fruit, you are sure to die."

—Genesis 2:15-17 NLT

\\\

For you are dust, and you will return to dust.

—Genesis 3:19 CSB

///

Know therefore today, and take it to your heart, that the Lord, He is God in heaven above and on the earth below; there is no other.

—Deuteronomy 4:39 NASB

\\\

The Lord brings death and makes alive; he brings down to the grave and raises up.

—1 Samuel 2:6 NIV

///

But now that the baby is dead, why should I fast? I can't bring him back to life. Someday I will go to him, but he cannot come back to me.

—2 Samuel 12:23 NCV

\\\

For You will not abandon my soul to Sheol; Nor will You allow Your Holy One to undergo decay. You will make known to me the path of life; In Your presence is fullness of joy; In Your right hand there are pleasures forever.

—Psalm 16:10-11 NASB

///

For all can see that the wise die, that the foolish and the senseless also perish, leaving their wealth to others. Their tombs will remain their houses forever, their dwellings for endless generations, though they had named lands after themselves.

People, despite their wealth, do not endure; they are like the beasts that perish …

But God will redeem me from the realm of the dead; he will surely take me to himself.

Do not be overawed when others grow rich, when the splendor of their houses increases; for they will take nothing with them when they die, their splendor will not descend with them.

—Psalm 49:10-12, 15-17 NIV

\\\

Nevertheless, I am continually with you; you hold my right hand. You guide me with your counsel, and afterward you will receive me to glory. Whom have I in heaven but you? And there is nothing on earth that I desire besides you.

—Psalm 73:23-25 ESV

///

Those who live in the shelter of the Most High will find rest in the shadow of the Almighty. This I declare about the Lord: He alone is my refuge, my place of safety; he is my God, and I trust him. For he will rescue you from every trap and protect you from deadly disease. He will cover you with his feathers. He will shelter you with his wings. His faithful promises are your armor and protection.

—Psalm 91:1-4 NLT

\\\

A person's life is like grass. Like a flower in the field it flourishes, but when the hot wind blows by, it disappears, and one can no longer even spot the place where it once grew.

—Psalm 103:15-16 NET

///

Precious in the sight of the Lord is the death of his saints.

—Psalm 116:15 KJV

\\\

For what happens to the children of man and what happens to the beasts is the same; as one dies, so dies the other. They all have the same breath, and man has no advantage over the beasts, for all is vanity. All go to one place. All are from the dust, and to dust all return.

—Ecclesiastes 3:19-20 ESV

///

The wolf also shall dwell with the lamb, and the leopard shall lie down with the kid; and the calf and the young lion and the fatling together; and a little child shall lead them.

And the cow and the bear shall feed; their young ones shall lie down together: and the lion shall eat straw like the ox.

And the sucking child shall play on the hole of the asp, and the weaned child shall put his hand on the cockatrice' den.

They shall not hurt nor destroy in all my holy mountain: for the earth shall be full of the knowledge of the Lord, as the waters cover the sea.

And in that day there shall be a root of Jesse, which shall stand for an ensign of the people; to it shall the Gentiles seek: and his rest shall be glorious.

—Isaiah 11:6-10 KJV

\\\

On this mountain he will destroy the burial shroud, the shroud over all the peoples, the sheet covering all the nations; he will destroy death forever. The Lord God will wipe away the tears from every face and remove his people's disgrace from the whole earth, for the Lord has spoken.

On that day it will be said, "Look, this is our God; we have waited for him, and he has saved us. This is the Lord; we have waited for him. Let us rejoice and be glad in his salvation."

—Isaiah 25:7-9 CSB

///

Good people pass away; the godly often die before their time. But no one seems to care or wonder why. No one seems to understand that God is protecting them from the evil to come. For those who follow godly paths will rest in peace when they die.

—Isaiah 57:1-2 NLT

\\\

Violence will not be heard again in your land, Nor devastation or destruction within your borders; But you will call your walls salvation, and your gates praise.

No longer will you have the sun for light by day, Nor for brightness will the moon give you light; But you will have the Lord for an everlasting light, And your God for your glory.

Your sun will no longer set, Nor will your moon wane; For you will have the Lord for an everlasting light, And the days of your mourning will be over.

—Isaiah 60:18-20 NASB

///

As I kept watching, thrones were set in place, and the Ancient of Days took his seat. His clothing was white like snow, and the hair of his head like whitest wool. His throne was flaming fire; its wheels were blazing fire. A river of fire was flowing, coming out from his presence. Thousands upon thousands served him; ten thousand times ten thousand stood before him. The court was convened, and the books were opened …

I continued watching in the night visions, and suddenly one like a son of man was coming with the clouds of heaven. He approached the Ancient of Days and was escorted before him. He was given dominion, and glory, and a kingdom; so that those of every people, nation, and language should serve him. His dominion is an everlasting dominion that will not pass away, and his kingdom is one that will not be destroyed.

—Daniel 7:9-10, 13-14 CSB

\\\

As for you, go your way until the end. You will rest, and then at the end of the days, you will rise again to receive the inheritance set aside for you.

—Daniel 12:13 NLT

About the Bible Translations

Grateful thanks and acknowledgments are given to the following copyright holders for the wonderful Bible translations used in the compiling of this book:

§§§

Scripture Index

Genesis

Exodus

Leviticus

Numbers

Deuteronomy

Joshua

Judges

1 Samuel

2 Samuel

1 Kings

2 Kings

1 Chronicles

2 Chronicles

Ezra

Nehemiah

Job

Psalms

Proverbs

Ecclesiastes

Isaiah

Jeremiah

Lamentations

Ezekiel

Daniel

Hosea

Joel

Amos

Jonah

Micah

Haggai

Zechariah

Malachi

About Mike Nappa

Mike Nappa is executive editor for the *Big Ideas from the Bible™* series and a practical theologian known for writing *Bible-Smart™: Matthew* and a number of "coffee-shop theology" books. He's a best-selling and award-winning author with millions of copies of his works sold worldwide.

Mike holds an M.A. in Bible and Theology from Calvin Theological Seminary, a second M.A. in English from the University of Northern Colorado, and a B.A. in Christian Education from Biola University.

An Arab-American, Mike is proud to be a person of color (BIPOC) active in Christian publishing.

Visit Mike's Bible-Smart blog at *Bible-Smart.com*